What is
Peace?

Barnabas
in
Schools

Text copyright © Chris Hudson 2014
Illustrations copyright © Simon Smith 2014
The author asserts the moral right
to be identified as the author of this work

Published by
The Bible Reading Fellowship
15 The Chambers, Vineyard
Abingdon OX14 3FE
United Kingdom
Tel: +44 (0)1865 319700
Email: enquiries@brf.org.uk
Website: www.brf.org.uk
BRF is a Registered Charity

ISBN 978 1 84101 691 7

First published 2014
10 9 8 7 6 5 4 3 2 1
All rights reserved

Acknowledgements
Unless otherwise indicated, scripture quotations are taken from the Contemporary English
Version of the Bible, published by HarperCollins Publishers, copyright © 1991, 1992, 1995
American Bible Society.

Scripture quotations taken from the Holy Bible, New International Version (Anglicised edition).
Copyright © 1979, 1984, 2011 by Biblica (formerly International Bible Society). Used by
permission of Hodder & Stoughton Publishers, an Hachette UK company. All rights reserved.
'NIV' is a registered trademark of Biblica (formerly International Bible Society). UK trademark
number 1448790.

Scripture quotations taken from the Holy Bible, Today's New International Version. Copyright
© 2004 by Biblica. Used by permission of Hodder & Stoughton, an Hachette UK company.
All rights reserved. 'TNIV' is a registered trademark of Biblica.

Scripture quotations taken from THE MESSAGE, copyright © by Eugene H. Peterson 1993, 1994,
1995. Used by permission of NavPress Publishing Group.

Cover illustration: © Simon Smith 2014

A catalogue record for this book is available from the British Library

Printed and bound by CPI Group (UK) Ltd, Croydon CR0 4YY

What Price Peace?

A teaching resource for primary schools
exploring issues of war and peace

Chris Hudson

Contents

Assemblies

*

Introduction

Why are we studying the First World War?

Primary schools don't usually cover the First World War (sometimes called the 'Great War') in History, but there are times when we have to make an exception. The 1914–1918 centenary will be marked in a variety of ways over the next four years, notably with a football match celebrating the famous one played in No Man's Land on Christmas Day in 1914. Explaining all this to our pupils will mean acquainting ourselves with an unfamiliar topic and searching for positive things to say and do about a chain of events that is usually seen as an international catastrophe. This book aims to help you find some of those positives, providing you with stories and lesson material to shed light on the beliefs and values that might still have relevance today.

Studying the First World War can induce several reactions. There might be admiration for the courage, good humour and resourcefulness of those caught up in it, and sympathy for those whose lives were ripped up and destroyed. There might be a sense of depression at the sheer wastefulness of what happened, which created a dark pattern for future conflicts. There could also be curiosity. What can we discover in these events about human beings, or about God? Each one of the stories in this book is intended to extend thinking about both these questions, in RE lessons and other subjects too.

How might it be relevant to our pupils?

We often speak of the desire for peace, but a quick look at history shows that when it comes to 'sorting things out' internationally, humanity prefers wielding the sword to the pen. Belgium, which saw much of the fighting in the First World War, was once satirically described as a country deliberately invented to be the place where the British, French and Germans could settle their differences.

Perhaps fighting a war is simpler. Achieving a consensus is usually difficult. Someone has to start the complex business of negotiation. 'Agreement' involves us having to listen to others, who then have to listen to us. Compromises might be reached, but then they have to be painstakingly followed through. It's so much easier just to throw rocks.

We still say we want peace in the world, especially around Remembrance Sunday. But what is 'peace'? Does it simply mean 'nothing much happening'? And how do we achieve it? 'Peace Studies' were once derided in the popular press, but anything giving serious thought to peace and reconciliation surely merits study, especially when there are so many recent examples of individuals and countries trying to solve their disputes without resorting to bombs or bullets. Indeed, the European Community was founded on this very principle, and has been amazingly successful. The fall of the Berlin Wall symbolised an 'impossible' reconciliation between people divided by the Cold War. South Africa and Northern Ireland represent further examples of warring communities that are slowly, painfully, achieving levels of peace. Miracles happen.

The Bible gives a mixture of possible reasons for all this. Within its pages, earlier voices often celebrate the power to wage war on God's behalf, sometimes urging it on with chilling enthusiasm. But as the story develops through the centuries, we hear new voices talking of a greater kingdom, not dependent on spears, bows or chariots; and at his arrest, Jesus said, 'Put your sword away. Anyone who lives by fighting will die by fighting' (Matthew 26:52).

Since then, Christians have been ambivalent about whether or not war is a Bad Thing. The conversion of the Roman emperor Constantine in AD312 made Christianity the European state religion and, therefore, a power player. Many wars were fought over politically correct understandings of what the Christian God apparently wanted from people within 'Christendom'. By the 19th century, 'Christian' Europe was quite happy to extend its reach and control into Asia and Africa, using levels of barbarity that would have been unthinkable back home, until the First World War reintroduced these methods into Europe and the Nazis later reinvented slavery for a modern age. Today, many of the West's current conflicts with the Islamic world result from a furious reaction against Christendom's global domination down the centuries.

And now? We continue to have armed forces serving around the world, many in extremely difficult circumstances. Despite the controversy at home, there is much talk of 'supporting our troops' and honouring their sacrifice in our service. Sir Cecil Spring Rice's old hymn 'I vow to thee, my country' sums up the paradox. The first verse is a patriotic, flag-waving celebration of dutiful sacrifice for our country, which is rather hard to sing these days, but the last verse speaks of 'another country' whose pride is in suffering and whose 'paths are peace'. This is the kingdom of God hinted at by Jesus in his parables, the one that grows like a mustard seed, starting from almost nothing, then expanding to shelter the whole world. It may be invisible but it's there at work in our homes, classrooms and playgrounds if we only have the eyes to see it, desire it and give it space to flourish. Peacemaking might cost a person everything, but, according to Jesus, it marks them out as a child of God.

How does this fit into Spiritual, Moral, Social and Cultural Education (SMSC)?

If you're not religious, what connection does RE have with 'real life'? Let's think a little wider. Moments of national significance (such as celebrations) can break down barriers and draw people together in a common cause—or, indeed, divide them. Anniversaries such as the centenary of the First World War provide opportunities to reflect on some important questions:

- What does it mean to be British? Is war ever justified? Why should we 'support our troops'?
- What should we do for the victims and survivors of war? How do we make peace?
- Is God ever on anyone's 'side'?

Questions like these have a great deal to do with shared and personal identity, moral reasoning and the nature of courage and compassion, and our answers to them will all be influenced by faith and belief. Religious Education becomes more relevant to the lives of our pupils as we relate it to issues raised in Citizenship or History. It raises the level of classroom discussion, too, because ignoring the world of faith and belief will impoverish any attempt to understand the decisions that people make. Handling 'real life' questions is crucial for SMSC, and thoughtful RE is well placed to support it.

How do we use this book?

What Price Peace? is part of a much larger project. There are further support materials available online for classroom teachers, an INSET programme and a series of creative Barnabas RE Days that can bring a specialist into your school to offer pupils a day's package of drama, storytelling and games to help them explore some of the themes introduced in this book. See www.barnabasinschools.org.uk/whatpricepeace/ for further details.

So how could this fit into your schemes of work? It depends on who has control of your History and RE curricula and the degree of creative freedom that your school is prepared to exercise. You could organise a special topic day, week or fortnight in which large parts of the curriculum in every class are given over to exploring different aspects of the First World War. Alternatively, you could plan for each class to experience at least one half-term's study on the theme, preferably in cross-curricular fashion, at some point over the next four years.

Which of the ten units of work are most appropriate for each year group? Have a read through, and decide for yourself. The unit on 'Woodbine Willie' ('Waiting for a train') is the one that works hardest to explore how Christian ideas about God and war changed as a result of the conflict. If time is short, you could select one from each of the following categories:

Patriotism and protest

- Rule Britannia! Keir Hardie faces a hostile patriotic crowd (page 17)
- Tooth and claw: Vernon Kellogg discusses reasons for fighting a war (page 63)
- The white feather: Stephen Hobhouse goes to prison (page 157)

Keeping yourself human

- Tommy's zoo: Tom Bennett finds a new pet (page 81)
- A hurricane of poetry: Fred Roberts gives soldiers a voice in *The Wipers Times* (page 95)

Caring for the soldiers

- 'Stretcher bearer!' William Coltman and Richard Tawney in No Man's Land (page 113)
- Waiting for a train: 'Woodbine Willie' and other military chaplains (page 127)
- 'Her face is the fairest': Nurses and VADs caring for the sick and wounded (page 143)

Myths and reality

- Answering the call: Vesta Tilley goes out recruiting (page 35)
- A whisper of wings: Arthur Machin creates a myth by accident (page 49)

If you are planning to run this as a whole-school topic, we strongly suggest that you use the first assembly ('How the "Great War" started') to provide context for the theme. One of the other two assemblies could be used to mark the conclusion.

Stories, extracts and illustrations can be downloaded free from www.barnabasinschools.org.uk/9781841016917/ together with a list of all the web links cited in this book for easy reference. Downloads are A4 sized.

A bonus 'What price peace?' story has also been added to the website, with extra cross-curricular activities for use in class with more able pupils. 'There and back again' retells the First World War experiences of J.R.R. Tolkien, author of *The Hobbit* and *The Lord of the Rings*. Tolkien's time in the army provided him with useful material for writing about the fantasy wars in Middle Earth, as well as much cause for personal reflection, as recounted in his letters.

Stories and lesson material

Rule Britannia!

*

Rule Britannia!
Keir Hardie faces a hostile patriotic crowd

Background for teachers

In early 1914, no one knew what a modern war would look like. Maxim 'machine' guns had been used to slaughter a Zulu army in Africa, barbed wire had successfully defended trenches from cavalry in the American Civil War, and authors like H.G. Wells had been dreaming up technology-driven science-fiction battles of the future, but all this was forgotten. The politicians and generals of Europe anticipated a series of fast-moving clashes between mobile armies led by waves of horse-mounted cavalry, and they expected the whole business to be 'over by Christmas'.

They were wrong. After a confused start, the 'Western Front' quickly became an area of war on the defensive, with the odds stacked against aggressive moves that might break the deadlock. It took four long years before new weapons and tactics (poison gas, explosive mines, aircraft, tanks and telecommunications), massed industrial output and the entry of the USA finally ended the conflict. By 1918, the remaining European powers, both victors and losers, were exhausted, broken and bitter. Little had been resolved, and the War to End All Wars… sadly *didn't*.

In August 1914, great excitement swept the British nation when war was declared, with much talk of renewed national purpose. Belgium (often depicted as a helpless female) had to be defended in accordance with the British sense of fair play, and serving one's country would be a powerful test of manhood. And since we were doing the decent and honourable thing, God would most definitely be on our side, wouldn't he? Naturally, much the same sort of thing was being said in Germany, except that God was, in their eyes, supporting the right of the German nation to defend itself against being hemmed in by the French, British and Russians. For many young people across Europe, war represented a chance to play the dashing hero and do one's bit for one's motherland or fatherland, and so they flocked to the recruiting offices, worried that it would all be over too soon.

Some, however, opposed the war from the very beginning. This was a lonely position to be in, and frequently dangerous. As MP for Merthyr Tydfil, Keir Hardie was a popular miners' leader, trade unionist, Christian and resolute pacifist, speaking out repeatedly in Parliament and elsewhere against anything that might escalate the impending conflict. Two days after war was declared, he went back to his constituency to speak at a long-planned meeting on 6 August—where things turned nasty.

STORY RETELLING: RULE BRITANNIA!

Keir Hardie strode up the high street from the railway station, enjoying the fresh air and exercise after being cooped up in the train for hours. It was good to be back in Wales, away from the craziness of London. Then he noticed the Union flags in the shop windows. So, there were people who supported the war here, too. He'd hoped things would be different back here. Still, they trusted him as their MP, didn't they? He'd stood by their coal miners when they'd demanded more pay and safer working conditions down the pits. That would still count for something, wouldn't it? Surely they'd listen to him now. Of course they would.

After leaving his bags with a friend, Keir went for a stroll around town, collecting his thoughts before the big peace meeting. This war with Germany was wrong but it could still be stopped, or Britain could at least keep out of it. Suppose people simply refused to join the army? Everybody could just say 'No' to the war, starting right here in Wales. The idea could spread across Europe. There was still time! He just needed to say the right words.

Approaching the huge, dark Aberdare market hall, Keir joined a large crowd of people filing in, some bearing flags. There were thousands already inside, all talking excitedly, some of them miners he'd supported, people he knew by name. So, he was among friends—excellent! This was his big chance. He'd tell them how crazy this war was, and how people could still make their voices heard. He walked to the front, joining the small group of supporters who'd helped him at the last election. But there was no Charlie, and that saddened him. Charles Stanton, the local miners' leader, had worked with him on so many campaigns but this time he'd sent a message to say he wasn't coming tonight, because 'I stand by my country.' So Charlie was for the war, not against it. Crazy!

It was nearly time for Keir to speak. 'Sweet Jesus,' he prayed quietly, 'help me to do your will and speak the truth. Blessed are the peacemakers, for theirs is the kingdom of God.'

He felt a hand on his shoulder. 'Mr Hardie?' He turned and looked up. It was Edmund Stonelake, who would be chairing the meeting. 'Mr Hardie, I think you need to know something before we start.'

'What's that?'

'I've been talking to some of them here before you arrived. The people round here… well, Mr Hardie, I have to say they are intensely *in favour* of this war.'

'Are you telling me that these good working people are in favour of fighting other working people?'

'If those others are Germans, then yes, Mr Hardie. There's a German baker in the town who's had his windows smashed. If I were you, I'd watch my words tonight.'

Another pat on the shoulder, then the chairman stepped up to the front. Keir mopped his forehead with a handkerchief. What now? What did Jesus do when he faced an angry crowd? Oh well. Blessed are the peacemakers.

But as soon as he stood up to speak, someone rang a bell and the crowd at the back started singing the National Anthem. 'GOD SAVE OUR GRACIOUS KING…' He waited until they finished, but as he opened his mouth again there were jeers. 'GO BACK TO GERMANY!' someone yelled.

This time, Keir kept talking. 'I'm here to talk about peace, and I'm here to talk about people. Our government seems determined to destroy that peace. And if things unfold as seems likely, then a great many of our people will suffer for that decision made two days ago, propelling us towards war. There are some here who do not want that message to be heard and are determined to silence me. I will not be silenced! Ten millions of men are marching from various points of the compass to shed each other's blood!'

'TRAITOR!' a woman shrieked. Then the bell rang again, and again they started singing the National Anthem, but he didn't stop this time. 'No one wants this war except the people who will make money out of it!' he bellowed. 'No one has been asked whether we even want to go to war! We should be keeping out of this mess!'

But there was more shouting as the crowd at the back

unfurled their Union flags and waved them together while singing, 'Rule, Britannia; Britannia rule the waves; Britons never, never, never shall be slaves!'

Keir was shouting even louder now. 'Fighting this war will not bring peace to Belgium!'

But someone shouted back. 'Jesus said, "I come not to bring peace but a sword!" And we are the sword of his righteous anger!'

Keir was furious. 'I do not think our Lord would be pleased to hear anyone speak so lightly of war! Why are we supporting the Tsar of Russia? He has workers' blood on his hands! We are nearer to the Germans than we are to Russia!'

'TRAITOR! GERMAN-LOVER!' shouted someone else. The angry stamping and shouting, the chanting and singing, were getting louder and louder. Then, BANG! A gun fired, and again. BANG! A woman screamed. A hand was grabbing his arm. 'Mr Hardie! This way!' The chairman was pulling him off the stage, dragging him towards a back door, but people were waiting outside, shouting and pushing and shoving him as he hurried with the chairman back down the street to the place where he was staying. And that wasn't the end of it. All night, the crowd were chanting slogans outside the house and singing their songs. 'TURN THE GERMAN OUT! TURN THE GERMAN OUT!'

Next day, as he caught his train, with policemen there to stop any more trouble, Keir was shaking his head. 'Why do they want this?' he wondered. 'Why won't they listen?' He remembered the story of Jesus in the garden of Gethsemane. Jesus was left all alone as his friends either turned on him or ran away. Was this how Jesus must have felt?

* * *

21

After telling this story, explain that although Keir Hardie kept campaigning against the war, very few people listened to him. He died a year later, exhausted and frustrated, on 26 September 1915. The First World War lasted for four years, and during its course about a million British people died.

Religious Education: Speaking out or keeping silent?

Age 5–7: When friends fail

What's it like to be in a place where lots of people are shouting, trying to persuade each other about who's right and who's wrong? Sit the class in a circle and, on a signal, get them to chant, 'YES! YES! YES!' as you turn on the spot, pointing to different children. Each time you point at a child, that child has to change what he or she is shouting to 'NO! NO! NO!' Try it in different ways (for example, using the words 'CUSTARD!' and 'JELLY!' or the names of local rival football teams), listening to the way the sound changes as there are more and fewer YESes and NOs. What does it feel like to be saying one thing when everyone else is saying something different?

When telling Keir Hardie's story, you will need to simplify it, perhaps re-enacting it as a simple drama, with groups of children primed to shout, 'God save the King!' or 'Rule Britannia!' as 'Keir Hardie' tries to talk some simple scripted words of peace to a crowd. At the end, ask how he must have felt to have been treated like this in a place where he thought he was among friends. What words would describe his feelings? (Try to move beyond 'sad', and ask the children to give reasons for their choice of words.)

Then, using an appropriate child-friendly Bible version, retell the story of Jesus at the last supper and the garden of Gethsemane (Mark 14:12–43, 66–72), emphasising how Jesus' friends had promised they'd always stick with him but then fell asleep, panicked, ran away or lashed out. One (Judas) betrayed him to the soldiers, while another (Peter) denied even knowing him.

Again, ask how Jesus would have felt. What similarities can we see between the two stories? You could also discuss how the crowds of Jesus' time started Holy Week shouting, 'HOSANNA!' but, by the end, were shouting, 'CRUCIFY!'. Perhaps play the shouting game again, using these words.

Friendship is a big issue for children at this age. Ask each child to draw a picture of themselves and a friend, listing next to it things that might break up the friendship and things that act as glue to keep them and their friend together.

Conclude by saying that Jesus did see his friends much later on, and was able to rebuild that friendship. They were very glad to see him. (You could look at Peter's conversation with Jesus by the lake in John 21:1–17.) Sadly, Keir Hardie didn't have a similar moment with his friend Charles. The war had broken up their friendship.

Age 8–11: With God on our side?

Throughout history, many political leaders have sought approval for their actions from heavenly powers. In the Bible, there's a curious moment when God's people try to literally drag him into a local war by taking the ark of the covenant with them on campaign. (This was a box containing the tablets of stone on which were inscribed the Ten Commandments—a box where they presumably thought God lived.) Two renegade apprentice priests accompanied it into battle against the enemy, and died when it was captured by the Philistines.

This lesson involves detailed study of a complex Bible story, so you will need to be selective in your use of a good child-friendly version when retelling the story. Your best approach might be through a drama lesson, using different groups of children to act out different parts. Retell the story in three parts, starting with the tale of an apprentice priest, Samuel, who is given a frightening message (1 Samuel 3:1–18). Pause to discuss: what questions do we have at this stage? (Note how Samuel listens to the Lord, when his elders don't.)

Then tell the second part of the story together, in which the ark (or 'sacred chest' in the Contemporary English Version) is taken into battle and lost (1 Samuel 4:1–22). Discuss what questions the different characters in the story (Samuel, Eli and his sons, the Philistines) might be asking at this point.

Move on to the third and last part, where the ark causes mayhem, both in the place it is taken to and the place it is returned to (summarise 1 Samuel 5:1–12; 6:1–20). At the end, discuss: what is this story saying about trying to drag God on to your side in a battle? Discuss the role of Eli, who allowed his sons to do such bad things when he was the one meant to be in charge.

As follow-up, ask pupils to draw the ark of the covenant (using prompts from Google Images), under the title 'God on our side?' Encourage them to show in thought bubbles what they think Eli's sons and their Philistine enemies would have been thinking when they took it into battle. In another thought bubble, ask them to write what they think God might have been thinking.

Literacy: What's the future going to be like?

No one in the Victorian or Edwardian era really knew what a modern war would be like, although some authors and artists tried to imagine it. The Victorian fascination with science and new technology created the genre of 'science fiction', which wondered about future possibilities, particularly in the stories of H.G. Wells and Jules Verne and the drawings of Albert Robida. Several children's authors today, such as Philip Reeves (*Mortal Engines*), and fantasy TV series such as *Doctor Who* still reference this faux-Victorian 'steampunk' genre, also exploring the darker uses to which technology can be put, such as creating terrifying weapons of war.

Age 5–7: Wonderful machines?

Using Google Images, access and show the class examples of the (peaceful) illustrations of Albert Robida. Look in particular at one of the flying machines. How does it work? What words could we use to describe it? Write and display the words as children suggest them, encouraging the use of technical language such as balloon, propeller, sails, anchor, and so on.

Explain that, over 100 years ago, many people were wondering what the future would be like, and drawings like these were very popular. Of course, though, inventions like these might also be used as weapons. Show images from Robida's *The 20th Century War*, drawn in 1883. What do we think of these—exciting, or scary?

Together, act out what it would be like to be riding in one of these flying war machines, pulling or pushing imaginary levers and buttons as you attack the enemy. Then come in to land—and see what you've done. Has anyone been hurt? What might you feel? Could we use this amazing invention for something that's more kind to people?

Alternatively, using one or more of these drawings as a stimulus, together create a vocabulary display to describe different parts of the machine. Add some words of wonder, or possibly fear. Then imagine you are a news reporter seeing it for the first time, perhaps at a public display: 'Today I have seen something amazing...' Describe it, talking about what you saw it do, but also wondering about what it might do if it was used as a weapon.

Age 8–11: Science fiction goes to war

By 1914, there were many anticipations of aerial warfare, floating fortresses and terrifying new weapons on the battlefield. Some of these ideas were completely wrong, but many of H.G. Wells' prophecies turned out to be partially correct. With your class, study selected passages from his story *The Land Ironclads*, which was written in 1903, anticipating the invention of tanks. This can be accessed online at: http://en.wikisource.org/wiki/The_Land_Ironclads. Although he supported the war, Wells thought it important to show the human consequences of conflict. The beginning of Chapter 3 describes the machines, and Chapters 2 and 4 describe the impact on soldiers fighting in trenches.

Alternatively, Jules Verne's *20,000 Leagues Under the Sea* chillingly describes an attack by a submarine on a warship in Chapter 21. (This is accessible free online at www2.hn.psu.edu/faculty/jmanis/julesverne/20000leagues.pdf.)

Ask the following questions:

• Are there any words and phrases conveying the author's feelings about what he describes?
• What does he think of this use of science and technology?

You could move into a wider discussion, considering questions such as:

• Are there inventions that you wish had never been invented?
• Why does so much effort and money go into creating weapons of war?
• Why do so many people find war stories and science fiction interesting?

Create heavily annotated drawings of the technology that Wells or Verne describes. What is each part of the machine designed to do? What would it feel like to be on the receiving end of one of these war machines? Write an imagined first-hand account from the point of view of a soldier or sailor being attacked by Wells' ironclad or Verne's submarine.

Extension

H.G. Wells' *The War of the Worlds* imagines a Martian attack on Edwardian England. Wells deliberately used this story to criticise British attitudes to colonised peoples, who were attacked with superior British technology such as machine guns. What would it be like for us to be on the receiving end of a superior race's ambitions? Read and discuss short extracts that focus on the shocking impact of powerful technology used to attack defenceless people.

History: Keir Hardie's peace meeting

Age 5–7: Thinking about the peace meeting

As suggested in the RE section, re-enact the scene in the meeting. Afterwards, discuss whether you would have wanted to be there. Why or why not? What were the most important things that people were saying about the war? What do you think the different people were feeling? What further questions would you be asking about what happened that night? List and display key points.

After the discussion, set an individual task entitled '1914: Should we go to war?' Ask pupils to draw (or stick in) a copy of the Union flag, surrounded by some faces and speech bubbles for different people at the meeting, showing what they were feeling. Finally, ask them to add: 'If I was there, I would say Yes/No, because…'

Age 8–11: Studying original newspaper reports

This is the original news report of Keir Hardie's meeting on 6 August 1914, from *The Aberdare Leader*. It can be downloaded from www.barnabasinschools.org.uk/9781841016917 at A4 size.

War against war—hostile reception of Mr Keir Hardie. Uproarious meeting at Aberdare

A meeting under the auspices of the Labour Party was held at the Aberdare market on Thursday last. There was a very large attendance, but the whole of the proceedings was of a most uproarious character. Councillor E. Stonelake presided, and was supported by Mr Keir Hardie MP, Mr T. Richardson MP, Councillor Idwal Thomas and others.

Councillor E. Stonelake opened the proceedings by stating that they had met under one of the gloomiest clouds that had ever overspread Europe. War had broken out, and it was essential for them to know something about it before so freely talking about it on street corners. Under the circumstances they ought to be grateful to Mr Keir Hardie and Mr Richardson for coming there, for the consequences to the working classes of the war were such as no one could measure. (Cheers)

Mr Keir Hardie then started to address the meeting, but was received with loud hooting, which was mingled with cheers. A large section of the crowd started singing, 'God Save Our Gracious King' and this was again followed by cheering. Then most of the crowd got up on chairs to have a better view of the meeting, and it was impossible to proceed. A few minutes elapsed and then a section of the audience again struck up 'Rule Britannia'. A slight lull followed, and Mr Keir Hardie was heard by the reporters present to say that the meeting was organised before war was declared.

After the declaration of the war, he had considered very seriously whether the meeting should be postponed.

At this stage the singing at the back of the hall recommenced, and it was almost impossible to hear the speaker. However, Mr Keir Hardie was understood to say he had decided to come, and that he had not a trace of the coward in his blood. (Cheers, mingled with groans.) Ten millions of men were marching from various points of the compass to shed each other's blood. (Continued uproar and singing of the National Anthem.) No one wanted the war but the Tory Press, and it was only after the statement by Sir Edward Grey that the Liberal Party found itself committed to war. It had been committed to war without even being consulted. He maintained that the proper attitude for this country ought to have been one of neutrality. (Loud hooting, followed by the singing of Rule Britannia.)

For several minutes it was quite impossible to hear Mr Hardie, the uproar being deafening. He was understood by those nearest to him to say that they should endeavour to remember the origins of war. Germany had made this country an offer, and instead of accepting Germany's offer, war was declared, and they were now in the field. They were now fighting for Russia. (A voice shouting 'Shame!' and great uproar.) Again a section of the audience sang the National Anthem, and the intensity of opposition to Mr Hardie increased.

In fact, it became evident that the meeting was soon to be broken up. Mr Hardie seemed to realise this, and after stating that there were awful times in store for the working classes of this and other countries, he concluded his address by saying that the Labour Party would continue to educate public opinion so that this dishonourable war should be brought to an end. The working classes all over Europe were working with them in the same direction. Mr Hardie then resumed his seat amidst cheers from his supporters, and the singing of Rule Britannia by the rest of the audience...

Just before the meeting was declared closed a number of shots were fired by some person at the back of the hall.

On departing, Mr Hardie was hustled by a number of people, and was followed through Victoria Square, Canon Street, and High Street by a large crowd, who every now and then gave vent to groans. On reaching the residence of Mr and Mrs Matt Lewis, in Elm Grove, with whom he was staying, Mr Hardie was again hooted. Mr Matt Lewis asked this crowd to disperse quietly, as he had a child in bed, but the crowd replied by singing, 'Turn the German out!' Eventually the crowd left, and an exciting experience for Mr Hardie came to an end.

* * *

- Highlight and work out the meaning of any unfamiliar words and phrases.
- What does this newspaper report tell you about opinions in Britain about the war on 6 August 1914?
- This news report was written at a time when almost all the newspapers were backing the war. Are there any clues in this piece about the opinions of the news reporter? Rewrite a short section of this report as if the reporter was either very pro-war or anti-war. Do this by using more 'loaded' adjectives and adverbs to show what you might think of Mr Hardie and the crowd.
- Compare this account with the fictional version. Make two lists to show what the modern author has included or left out in the story, to help make it understandable for a modern school audience. Having now studied the newspaper report, would you change anything in the story to improve it? (Note: for dramatic effect, the story includes a reference to Union flags in shop windows, a German-owned shop window being smashed, and Charles' absence being explained to Keir Hardie before the meeting. There is no historical evidence for any of these particular events on that night, although all are possible. Charles actually sent a message explaining his absence to Keir *after* the meeting.)
- If you could interview anyone who was there that evening, who would it be and what further questions would you ask about what happened?

Extensions

- Find out more about the life and work of Keir Hardie, presenting findings as a report of around 100–150 words. What were the most important issues he campaigned about?
- Turn the story and news report into a short playscript for a class to perform in assembly.

Personal and Social Education/Citizenship/ Circle Time: Letting others lead you

Age 5–7: Thinking about the 'herd instinct'

Explain that the Keir Hardie story shows what can happen if people don't ask enough questions but simply join in with what others are doing. Play the drama game of 'Billy's trousers'. Ask for three volunteers to stand next to you. Say that you are going to accuse each of them of 'stealing Billy's trousers', and they have to react without speaking but showing that they think they are totally innocent. Afterwards, say that no one likes getting into trouble. Sometimes, if they're caught doing something wrong, people will say, 'It's not my fault... it's someone else's fault.' Ask if they remember what that's called. *('Passing the buck.')*

Ask: 'Who here has ever been caught up in trouble with someone else, and afterwards couldn't work out who started it?' This happens when crowds of people get excited. Someone starts doing something, others join in, and finally everybody's doing it. At this point, have a volunteer (briefed in advance) point at a corner of the ceiling where there are no obvious features, saying, 'Can you see it?' See who copies them. Then ask, *was* there anything there? Explain that the urge to copy others is sometimes called the 'herd instinct', because people follow each other like a herd of sheep. Usually, it makes sense to copy what others are doing, but, if you let the wrong people lead you, then it gets you into trouble.

Role-play in threes: two people trying to persuade the third to do something wrong (for example, cheating in a test, taking someone else's things). What arguments do they use to persuade the third person? Which are the best ways to answer them? Share some of the role-plays and comment on the better ways of responding.

THOUGHT FOR THE DAY

Show a piece of Plasticine® or Blu-Tack®. Squeeze it and stretch it into different shapes. Say that in the Bible, a man named Paul said something like this: 'Don't let the world squeeze you into the shape it wants!' When do we become a little like this squeezable stuff?

Prayer

Father God, you made me with the ability to make good decisions. Help me not to let others make bad decisions for me. Amen

— UNIT 2 —

Answering the call:
Vesta Tilley goes out recruiting

Background for teachers

During the summer and autumn of 1914, thousands of young men across Europe dashed out to join the armed forces, excited by the prospect of getting into uniform and serving their country. British recruitment campaigns were especially successful. Many original diaries mention the powerful effect of the Lord Kitchener posters saying, 'Your country needs you!' with the finger that seemed to point at you wherever you stood. Others mention (with anger) the enthusiastic young women who gave white feathers to any young man seen out on the street but not in uniform, to tell them they were being cowards.

After the war, many veterans spoke with pride of the service they'd given their country. Of the 5.7 million men who served in the British Army during the First World War, nearly half were volunteers. (Conscription didn't start until 1916.) There were also remarkable levels of volunteer recruitment from the wider British Empire, such as the 50,000 soldiers from the Indian subcontinent who served in the trenches of the Western Front.

In Britain itself, there was great enthusiasm to join and 'do one's bit'. On the first day of the appeal for volunteers to join Lord Kitchener's New Army (7 August 1914), the crowd of men outside one central recruiting office in London was so large and boisterous that it took mounted police to keep them under control. Many volunteers joined as groups, becoming 'Pals' battalions such as the Church Lads Battalion (16/Kings Royal Rifle corps), the Sportsmen's Battalion (23/Royal Fusiliers) and local town formations like the famous Accrington Pals (11/East Lancashire). Once trained, many of these men had their first taste of modern warfare in July 1916 during the Battle of the Somme, which resulted in 57,470 casualties on its first day.

STORY RETELLING: ANSWERING THE CALL

'Britain's best recruiting sergeant' was a woman. 'Vesta Tilley' (Matilda Alice Powles, 1864–1952) was a variety artist who specialised in comic songs, cross-dressing as 'Burlington Bertie' and 'Tommy in the Trench'. When war broke out, she and her husband ran their own army recruitment drive, pulling together other artistes to create a series of shows across the country. Vesta performed songs like 'The army of today's all right' and 'Jolly good luck to the girl who loves a soldier', with recruitment officers on hand (frequently on stage) to sign up volunteers.

This imagined letter is based on a real incident in 1914.

Dear Miss Tilley,

I'm writing to you to tell you what I think about your performance at the variety show last week at the Palace Theatre. I was there with my husband Edward and his friend Jack who came over from Canada to serve in the war. We were all having a good night out when you came on in that beautiful gold dress and did some of your famous songs.

But then they opened the curtains behind you on stage, and there in front of a big Union flag was a line of soldiers in uniform, saluting us. And then they each of them sat down at a desk, waiting to enlist anyone who came up on stage. You got us all singing 'Rule Britannia', 'We don't want to lose you but we think you ought to go' and all those kinds of things.

Then you came off the stage and walked all round the audience singing your songs, up and down, both sides, down the middle—and all those young men were getting up and following you, one by one, with people cheering as they stood up to do it. Then you came to our row, and stopped at the end. My husband Edward was sitting there, and you put your hand on his shoulder, and you looked down at him as you sang a verse of your song. And then, when you'd moved off along the aisle, singing more of your song, he got up and followed you with all the others. You led those young men all up on stage to get enlisted as soldiers of the King, and everybody applauded and sang 'Land of hope and glory', and I was crying my eyes out.

Eddie and me, we've only been married a year. We've only just sorted out our house and our jobs, and we're planning to have a family and everything and we're working really hard for it. But now you took my husband with your singing and got him signed up as a soldier. When we got home that night I was crying and sobbing. I didn't want to lose him. I didn't want him to go at all. I said all of that to him, but he said, 'We have to go, Kathy. There has to be men to go.'

Miss Tilley, I hope you're proud of yourself. Because if he doesn't come back at the end of all this, it'll be your fault.

Yours sincerely,

Kathleen Ingleby

* * *

Discuss this letter with the class. Do they agree with Kathleen's last comment? Explain that this letter is based on a real incident, recounted in Kitty Eckersley's reminiscences in *Forgotten Voices of the Great War*. After being recruited into the army at the concert, Kathleen's husband was killed later on in the war, when she was pregnant with their first child. Vesta Tilley retired from the stage in 1920. Her husband was knighted for services to the war effort and later became an MP. On his retirement, they both left Britain to live in Monte Carlo, a small tax-haven principality on France's Mediterranean coastline.

Religious Education: Joining the fight

Age 5–7: 'Nothing to fear but fear itself'

The Bible contains a curious story about one man recruiting a resistance army to fight invaders and being told by God that the army is far too large (Judges 6—8). He has to carefully filter out the unsuitable, sending home the frightened and the careless, reducing his unwieldy horde to a small, committed commando force who subsequently defeat a much larger army through faith, good use of intelligence, fascinating strategy and a cool sense of courage. It's an interesting contrast to the mass recruitment of the First World War.

Begin the session by discussing fear. What is fear and how can it be useful (for example, helping us to avoid trouble and prevent accidents)? Develop the discussion by asking if there are times when overpowering fear can spoil things (for example, if we are scared of taking risks or trying something new). Explain that fear is natural, and real courage comes not from having no fear but rather from learning to understand and handle our fears. (People who have no fear at all can be rather dangerous. Can you think why?)

Share the Bible story of Gideon (Judges 6—8), using a suitable children's version. Afterwards, discuss his initial fears (threshing corn in secret, his repeated requests for confirmation of God's words), and how, when he put together his army, not everyone was suitable. Many were called, but few were chosen—but, in the end, this led to a stunning victory.

Follow up by asking pupils to draw or write about the things that they fear, adding an illustration of Gideon's broken jar with a flame inside, next to a sword and a trumpet. Encourage them to copy out the verse 'The Lord is with you, mighty warrior' (Judges 6:12, CEB). Ask the children to mark out one personal fear they'd like to address at some point. Encourage them to talk it through with a responsible adult if they wish. (This exercise may suggest material for further RE lessons or Circle Time sessions if any shared fears emerge.)

Age 5–7: Persuasion

Persuasion isn't wrong in itself but, by playing on the emotions, it can sway a person's judgment. Aesop tells a story about the sun and the wind conspiring to make a man remove his coat. The blustering wind fails, but the sun succeeds by making the weather too hot for thick clothes. In other words, there's more than one way to persuade people to do something, and Vesta Tilley's songs and flags and 'hand on the shoulder' put many young men into uniform who might otherwise have held back. Discuss TV adverts with your class. What sort of tricks do advertisers use to make children want the latest 'must-haves'? Show a few, and discuss elements such as music, clever words, cartoon characters or celebrities, use of graphics, and so on.

Set up a debate about the best use of a class reward. Shall we spend it as 'Golden Time', playing indoors or, instead, go outside? Encourage children to say what they think, and take a vote. Afterwards, discuss which arguments were the most persuasive and why.

The Barnabas website offers some interesting material about having personal goals, avoiding distractions and staying on task: see www.barnabasinschools.org.uk/staying-on-task/.

Age 8–11: The trouble with kings

Towards the end of the time of the Judges (such as Gideon and other leaders), the tribes of Israel decided they wanted a warrior king who would lead them into battles, so that they could be 'just like all the other nations' (1 Samuel 8:5). The prophet Samuel finally gave in, after passing on a chilling warning from the Lord that the people's wish for a monarchy in their quest for military success would end up with the pointless sacrifice of their children (which, if you know your biblical history, is how things turned out).

Begin the lesson by asking what makes a good leader. In groups, list the qualities that the class think would be needed to lead a sports team, an Antarctic exploration team, or a charity supporting a hospital, and report back. What sorts of qualities wouldn't they want to see in that kind of leader? Discuss.

Introduce the Bible passage (1 Samuel 8:1–22) by explaining that, at this point in their history, the Jewish people were a network of tribes, each having their own territories and leaders but sharing in the worship of the Lord, who had the prophet Samuel as his priest. One day, the tribal leaders came to Samuel, demanding that he choose a king to lead them into battle. Together, discuss the qualities they might have been looking for in a tribal warlord. Then read the passage in a suitable child-friendly version. Afterwards, note down any interesting questions from the pupils. Point out Samuel's warnings about what a king would do, and the Lord's sadness at being replaced.

Discuss what this story might have to do with the recruitment of soldiers for the First World War. Is there a distinction between defending one's nation and active empire-building? Draw out the dangers of choosing a leader who does not care for the people under their authority. Afterwards, set the task of copying this sentence: 'We want a king to rule us and lead us in battle' (1 Samuel 8:19). Next to it, ask pupils to list or draw three possible consequences of choosing a leader to fight your battles for you.

Extension

Write what you think might happen next in the story, then read on and discover what did happen next. (Saul was chosen as a reluctant king.) Are you surprised? Are there any interesting new questions?

Literacy: Persuading people to join up

Age 5–7: Songs of the First World War

Patriotic war songs were a powerful recruiting tool and were also used to keep columns of marching soldiers in step. Rousing songs might be sung back home, but soldiers on active service tended to prefer something more sentimental and light-hearted. Together, learn to sing at least one of the soldiers' songs from the First World War, with added percussion. Examples are 'Tipperary', 'Goodbye Dolly Grey' and 'Pack up your troubles in your old kitbag'. (An internet search will provide lyrics and tunes.)

Afterwards, display and study the lyrics for rhyme schemes, metre, and unusual words and their meanings. Discuss what you think soldiers and their families liked about the songs. Note the 'marching' beat, when it happens. Try singing while marching on the spot. Does it help you to sing or march better?

Age 8–11: Imagined correspondence

How do you think Vesta Tilley might have replied to Kathleen's letter? How might she have justified her recruitment campaign? With a partner, list some of the possible reasons that would have led a popular singer to use her talent to encourage young men to become soldiers. Then write the letter.

(In August 1914, many people thought that the main reason for Britain to enter the war was to save the Belgian and French people from the German army. They also thought that the war would be over by Christmas.)

Art: Sending a message

Age 5–11: Studying propaganda posters

In the course of the First World War, each country needed to grow a large army rapidly, developing their own series of recruitment campaigns to create a flood of patriotic volunteers. Each poster was carefully crafted to attract and influence a particular audience.

With your pupils, compare three or more First World War propaganda and recruiting posters from different countries. Google Images will provide a rich variety, but check that the historical period is correct, and avoid those of the extreme racist variety that play on negative national stereotypes. Good British examples include 'What did you do in the war, Daddy?', 'The Empire needs men' or 'Men of Britain! Will you stand this?' Use 'Google Translate' if necessary to understand the text of other languages. Compare the posters for their use of colour, images and motifs (including proportion), text type, text content and other features. Compile a list of adjectives that each one uses to make the audience feel in a certain mood. Which posters do you think are the most powerful, and why?

Using these ideas, set the task of designing a new First World War poster that encourages children and young people either not to waste food or to raise money to look after wounded soldiers.

History: Preparing soldiers for the trenches

Age 8–11: Briefing the troops

Using Google Images, source a selection of pictures from the First World War. Choose images that portray significant elements of trench life on the Western Front, such as a soldier in battle dress, barbed wire, a machine gun, and so on.

Set pupils, in teams, the task of imagining that they are officers in charge of training a bunch of new recruits who will soon be facing the trenches for the first time. They have 3–5 minutes to explain what it will be like, using the pictures as prompts to give three or four pieces of useful advice for working as a team and staying alive. They may also want to explain what happens in an attack.

Most pupils will probably prefer to script their presentations, but direct them away from just reading the script towards talking directly to the audience, perhaps using a few headings as cues. One useful kinaesthetic technique is to construct a mental list of points to go with each picture, counting them off on fingers as they are delivered. Planning for this might be done on a worksheet created by drawing around two hands.

Personal and Social Education/Citizenship/ Circle Time: Having a sense of responsibility

Many volunteers signed up to join the armed forces in the First World War, sharing a sense of responsibility for their nation. Their courage is easily forgotten. Use this as an opportunity for pupils to reflect on what it means to sacrifice our personal hopes and ambitions for something greater than ourselves.

Age 5–7: What is responsibility all about?

Ask, 'Who's heard the story of Peter Pan?' (Recount some key plot details, drawing out the fact that Peter Pan is the boy who never grows up.) Describe the very sad part at the end of the original story when Peter comes back to play with the children, only to find that they've all grown up. He's trapped because he's never going to grow up. Ask, 'Who *here* wants to grow up?' (Ask for a show of hands.) Ask why, and get pupils to discuss in pairs and feed back. What are the three main things they're looking forward to being able to do when they're grown up?

Explain that growing up isn't just about getting bigger and older. It's also about learning to become responsible. This morning, what did they have to do when they got up? What things do they have to do when they come to school?

In exercise books, set the task of listing or drawing 'My responsibilities', both 'now' and 'in future'. Afterwards, feed back, then ask what the connection is between the two lists. (As we get older, we're trusted to do more things. People who can handle them well then get trusted with *more* things, because they've got a greater sense of responsibility.)

Finish by saying that growing up is about learning how to handle responsibility. That can be a bit scary. Some people don't like making choices: they prefer to have someone else around to make their decisions for them, who can then be blamed when things go wrong. That can go badly if we let someone silly make our decisions for us. If you want to grow up well, you need to think about what you're responsible for, and do it well—or you might be a little like Peter Pan!

THOUGHT FOR THE DAY

Imagine yourself doing something when you're older, something that others are trusting you to do well. What are you going to do today to help you become that person in future?

Prayer

Father God, thank you that we can grow older and wiser and cleverer every day. Amen

Age 8–11: Having a sense of personal responsibility

Play the detective game (best done with children sitting in a circle). Send three 'detectives' just outside the door, with a 'minder' by the door to call them in. Set up a pattern of behaviour that everyone has to copy (for example, patting knees). Appoint a child as the 'leader', who is responsible for setting up new patterns of behaviour that everyone has to copy, but without being spotted by the detective while they are doing it. The minder then invites one detective into the middle of the circle, and allows them three attempts to spot the leader. Repeat with other leaders and detectives.

What helped the detectives to spot the leader? (Perhaps, for example, following the direction of other people's eyes.) In discussion, explore the different responsibilities of everyone in the game, pointing out that some responsibilities were personal and some were shared. In school, which responsibilities do you share with the other children in the classroom, and which are yours alone? Discuss in pairs, then list or draw them in exercise books under the headings 'My responsibilities' and 'Shared responsibilities'. Feed back afterwards, using this time to highlight 'grey areas' in classroom routines and re-establish forgotten ones.

Ask, 'When is it difficult to work out whose responsibility something is?' (When there's a job that no one wants to do, when there's a mess or a mistake that no one admits to making, and so on.)

With the whole group, point out that sometimes we just need to take on a difficult responsibility because no one else has the ability to do it. Highlight and praise children who tidy up without being asked, or don't just 'do their bit' but do a lot more for others. Say that these are the children who know a bit more about growing up, because they are showing a sense of responsibility. In the First World War, many people joined the army and volunteered to serve in other ways, because they didn't think they could leave it for others to do. For many, taking on this responsibility was a sign of growing up.

THOUGHT FOR TODAY

How grown-up do I want to be?

Prayer

Father God, I'm here as part of a class. We're all special here, but I'm responsible for my bit of it. Today, please show me how I can play my part better. Amen

A whisper of wings

*

A whisper of wings:
Arthur Machin creates a myth
by accident

Background for teachers

Myths can be dangerous. Once they have been proved untrue, people refuse to be fooled again—as in 'The boy who cried wolf'. Tales of German atrocities in the First World War (some partly true) were so exaggerated by Allied propagandists that no one with any sense believed in them. Unfortunately, similar (but worse) accounts of Nazi persecution were then disbelieved 20 years later, when they were actually true.

This unit of work looks at the true story of how a popular myth of the First World War got started. Arthur Machin's fictional story 'The bowmen' sparked off a wide-ranging popular folktale about British soldiers receiving supernatural help in battle, especially from the 'angels of Mons'. It's an opportunity to explore the slippery issues of faith and truth-telling with children: in whom, or what, do we place our trust? And, of course, are we ourselves trustworthy? Arthur Machin's own conclusions about faith and belief are well worth considering. You can read his own account of the 'angels of Mons' affair at www.aftermathww1.com/bowmint1.asp.

As a journalist, Arthur Machin would have probably agreed with another Christian writer, G.K. Chesterton, who allegedly said, 'When people stop believing in God, they don't believe in nothing—they'll believe in anything.'

STORY RETELLING: A WHISPER OF WINGS

Arthur Machin was completely baffled. He had only written a short story for a newspaper. It wasn't even a good story, because there had been a much better story in his head to start with, but this was the one that he finally set down on paper, then sent in to be printed. Now, something had gone wrong.

It was 1914, the early days of the First World War. A small British army was fighting bravely in the fields of Belgium, but the invading German army seemed to be winning, beating them back. It wasn't meant to be happening like this. So many British people had been cheering and waving flags when war was declared, but they weren't cheering now. On a hot Sunday morning in late August, Arthur read the reports in his newspaper, and they sounded grim. So many British soldiers had been killed in the retreat near the town of Mons. Their troops were pulling back, trying to save themselves from being overrun as the vast German army marched steadily forward. Was it unstoppable?

Later that morning, Arthur was still thinking about the news as he sat in church, waiting to go up for the Communion bread and wine. As a journalist, he was always looking for ideas, and his mind suddenly pictured the British soldiers killed in battle, lining up to be welcomed into heaven. He smiled sadly, then sat up, excited. What a story that could make! His newspaper would probably print it and perhaps he could give some comfort to the families of soldiers who had died. Yes, he thought, I'll write it all down this afternoon... after lunch. That delay was his big mistake.

By the time he actually put pen to paper, the story in Arthur's head had changed, as stories often do if you leave them for a bit. His new tale described a group of British soldiers standing in their trenches at night, bravely preparing to defend themselves against the thousands of powerful German soldiers marching towards them. Suddenly (in the story), strange archers in ancient armour appeared, letting fly a shower of arrows at the Germans, who turned and retreated in terror. In this fantasy story, the archers were the ghosts of Henry V's English army who had fought the battle of Agincourt nearby, long ago.

Shaking his head, Arthur laid down his pen. The story wasn't his best but it would have to do. He'd write something better when he had more time. The story was typed up, sent in to his editor for approval and, after a few days, 'The bowmen' appeared in the *London Evening News* for 29 September 1914, next to the latest news reports about the war. But when he came to read it, Arthur spotted a printing error. The newspaper layout people hadn't titled 'The bowmen' as 'a short story', so his tale read like a real news report—only with ghosts in it. Oh dear. Then, a few days after the story was published, editors from weekly magazines got in touch to ask if the story was true, and if they could reprint it. 'No, it's not true,' replied Arthur, slightly baffled, 'but of course you can reprint it if you pay for it!' They did, and so 'The bowmen' was reprinted. More magazines asked for permission to reprint the story, and the magazines sold out.

Six months later, a priest asked Arthur, 'Can I reprint your story as a pamphlet to give out to people on the street?'

'But why?' replied Arthur. 'You do know it didn't really happen, don't you? I made it all up!'

'What? But it must be true!' said the priest, looking puzzled. 'You just dressed it up a bit!'

'I didn't!' Arthur replied. 'It's just a story!' The priest was shocked. Everybody in his church had read 'The bowmen' and thought it was a real war report.

What was happening? Arthur's story was like a little snowball rolling down a hill, picking up speed and growing bigger and bigger. People were asking him about small details of 'The bowmen', saying that they knew the places he'd made up in his head. New stories uncannily like his own were being written and printed in newspapers and magazines. Somebody said that dead German soldiers had been found on the battlefield, shot by mysterious arrows. Somebody else mentioned a strange supernatural 'cloud' that appeared on the battlefield, hiding British soldiers from the enemy. St George had been seen on the battlefield, and angels, too! Yes, people were sharing stories of real angels that had been seen protecting the British soldiers from the Germans near the town of Mons. The letters pages were full of it. Friends of friends of soldiers said, yes, they'd seen the angels too.

'But I made it all up!' Arthur said to anyone who would listen. 'It's *just a story*!' He tried tracking down the so-called eyewitnesses. They all turned out like this: someone (unknown) had met a nurse (unnamed) who had talked to a soldier (unnamed as well) who had seen angels on the battlefield, the famous 'angels of Mons'. Everybody wanted to believe in the angels. A year later, along came another request from a publisher: could 'The bowmen' be reprinted as a small book, and would Arthur write an introduction for it? Arthur smiled: 'With pleasure!' At last he could explain to everybody that there had never been any angels. He set to work.

'So far,' he wrote, 'nothing remotely approaching proof has been offered as to any supernatural intervention during the retreat from Mons.'

As he went on, Arthur didn't say that there were no such things as angels. As a Christian, he was quite willing to believe in them. However, there was no evidence that they had appeared on the battlefield near Mons. But he had a question: why did so many people *want* to believe in the angels of Mons? Why was his story accepted so easily as fact, when it wasn't? That was a puzzle that needed a good answer, because so many people had believed a tale that was completely made up.

Arthur concluded that the people of his time, including those in the church, had given up believing in the supernatural God of the Bible, but they were still hungry for something mysterious and powerful. So, instead of believing in God, they were prepared to believe in just about anything else that might be supernatural, whether it made sense or not, and even if it sounded completely mad. That's what Arthur thought about the 'angels of Mons'. What do *you* think?

Religious Education: Whispering about wings

Age 5–7: The power of words

The letter of James in the Bible includes a warning about what happens when people misuse words (James 3:1–8). Games such as 'Chinese whispers' illustrate how a message can be changed as it is whispered from ear to ear. Discuss how the things that people say can change the way we feel about something. Display a nice-looking thing to eat and ask, 'Would you like to eat it?' Then add a 'fact' that might change people's minds (for example, it's made of powdered worms). A little thing like a word really can be important.

Ask everyone to stick out their tongue, to wiggle it around and feel it. Then say that it's one of the most powerful bits of your body. What nice things can we say to people? What nice things have other people said to us? How did that make us feel? Then tell Arthur Machin's story in an appropriate way, with everyone posing in statues to show how the story he wrote changed as people passed it on—from ghostly archers... to a mysterious cloud... to St George (a knight with a sword and a shield)... to powerful angels. His words were changed because everyone added their own bit.

Use one or more visual images (a ship's rudder, a horse's bridle, or fire) inspired by the letter of James to illustrate the idea that words can affect other people's lives and take on a life of their own. Together, discuss and list some kind words and phrases that we can all try to use with each other this week.

Age 5–7: Angels

Ask your pupils to list and draw their ideas of what they think an angel looks like. Explain that, around the world, there's a vast folklore about angels but in this country we tend to link them with Christmas. (In the class, which children have appeared as angels in a nativity play? What did they wear?) However, in the Bible, angels appear either as God's secret agents, bearing messages of good news, encouragement and even warnings, or as powerful beings who protect God's people when they are feeling lost or frightened.

Share the story of Elisha and the Aramaean army (2 Kings 6:8–23). Nowadays, the 'horses and chariots of fire' are thought to be a reference to angels. (Your class might need to be shown a picture of a chariot.) Afterwards, ask your class to discuss the story in pairs. What are the most interesting questions they can think of about it? (Questions can start with 'What? Who? Where? How? When?' or even 'I wonder...') Collect their responses. Explain that this story was probably written down at a time when God's people were living as prisoners in a place far away from their own homeland, where they were often frightened of being bullied. What do you think the message of the story might be?

Set the task of copying the line from the story, 'Lord, please help him to see' (v. 17), then illustrating what the servant might have seen. Afterwards:

- Write about a time when you were frightened and something helped you not to be scared.
- Design your own imagined angel of protection. Label different parts of the drawing. What is the angel's name?

Age 8–11: What is faith?

'Faith is being sure of what we hope for and certain of what we do not see' (Hebrews 11:1, NIV 1984).

Discuss with the class whether or not they believe the following statements, and why:

- The earth goes around the sun (true)
- Fire-breathing dragons used to live on our planet (not true)
- Jesus was born in a stable (no evidence)

Explain that unless we have our own direct evidence that something is true, we have to rely on other people to help us 'know' certain things, but that we should still be careful. All scientists agree about the first two statements above (true and not true), but the Bible makes no mention of a stable in the nativity stories. It only says that the baby Jesus was placed in a manger because there was no room in the inn. The concept of a stable came later, but there's no proof for it at all. However, lots of people like the idea of the stable, so most people's notions of the nativity include it. (Does your class think that matters? Why or why not?)

Christians believe that the Bible is a reliable guide to under-standing God, but they still have to use their minds to work out what God might be saying through the Bible's words, to apply it to their own lives. Read a Bible story about an angelic appearance, such as the annunciation (Luke 1:26–38) or something more martial such as the angel of death that wipes out an army in Isaiah 36:1–2, 13–21 and 37:21–22, 33–37.

Ask your class to discuss the story in pairs. What are the most interesting questions they can think of about it? Log their responses. Explain that a story like this can't be proved true or false, but it can still be very important to Christians because of what it says about God and his people. What powerful messages do you think it contains about strength and weakness, pride and humility?

Afterwards, set pupils the task of writing about their own beliefs concerning angels. (For those who don't believe, do they think it matters whether people believe in angels, or not?) Incidentally, why are so many people more interested in fantasy figures like vampires and werewolves than in stories of angels? Discuss.

For further discussion

Consider the following statements about belief. What does your class think?

- 'It doesn't matter what you believe as long as you are sincere.' (You could be sincerely prejudiced… and wrong!)
- 'You should only believe in something you can see for yourself.' (Can everything be proved like this—love, for example?)
- 'Trust no one.' (What could go wrong for someone who believes this?)

If somebody were to tell you that they had witnessed a supernatural event, perhaps claiming to have seen a ghost, what questions would you want to ask to help work out the truth?

'When people stop believing in God, they don't believe in nothing—they'll believe in anything.'

G.K. CHESTERTON (1874–1936)

Literacy: Traditional tales (old and new)

Age 5–7: Rewriting traditional tales

Many traditional 'fairy' tales take illusion and twisting-of-truth as their subject matter. After telling the story of the angels of Mons, share one or more of the following tales with the class:

- The boy who cried 'wolf'
- Chicken Little ('The sky is falling!')
- The emperor's new clothes

What do the messages in these stories have in common with what happened to Arthur Machin's story? Set pupils the challenge of rewriting one of these traditional stories (all easily found on the internet), giving the story a modern setting. (Might Chicken Little end up in a fast-food restaurant?)

Age 8–11: Using urban myths as a basis for creative writing

Why do you think so many people thought Arthur's story was true? 'The angels of Mons' is one example of an urban myth or legend. These 'friend of a friend' stories are popular tales passed on from person to person, often claimed as true but impossible to prove. Many urban myths are modern versions of much older traditional stories or even fairy tales, often taking a popular belief or fear as their subject matter.

One classic urban myth is 'The vanishing hitchhiker'. In this story, a motorist picks up a hitchhiker (usually at night) whose conversation, as they travel on, becomes increasingly odd until the moment when they pass on to the driver an important message and then disappear. Ask your class to write their own atmospheric version, using all their powers of description to build up the tension and create a powerful 'all-important message'.

Extension

Nowadays, the internet is a ready source of conspiracy theories and urban myths. Do you think a story like 'The angels of Mons' could be passed around today? How? Where might the story take place? Write a spoof newspaper account of an urban myth set in a modern place of conflict where soldiers are serving. Be careful to include enough believable detail to fool your reader into thinking it might be true.

History: Remembrance and folklore in 1914

Age 5–7: Images of remembrance

Introduce the idea of remembrance by visiting a local war memorial that lists the names of servicemen killed in the First World War. Point out any relevant imagery (poppies, angels, knights in armour, swords) or texts used on the memorial. Take photos of the names. During the visit, retell the story of how poppies started growing in the battlefield mud, and talk about how poppies are used today to remember the soldiers who died in the war.

Back in school, show a copy of Lord Kitchener's famous 'Your country needs you' poster. How do pupils think people would have felt when they saw the finger pointing at them? Discuss how local people would have been both excited and frightened when their sons or brothers or fathers went marching off to war in 1914, and how anxious they might have been when they heard that things weren't going well. Show a few suitable images of a soldier's life in the First World War, then retell 'A whisper of wings' in your own words, as appropriate for the age group. Afterwards, ask pupils why they think so many people believed Arthur's story was true or wanted it to be true.

Afterwards, create a 'war memorial' wall display of artwork related to the First World War, including poppies (made from red tissue paper and green wire), names of servicemen, and so on.

Age 8–11: Studying original source materials

'The angels of Mons' is a classic example of First World War folklore. With a partner, read a copy of 'The bowmen', Arthur Machin's original supernatural tale (see www.aftermathww1.com/bowmen.asp).

Highlight unfamiliar words and phrases and use a dictionary to discover their meanings. Then retell the story in about 50 words, using short sentences.

Arthur's story described ghosts protecting the British soldiers. Why do you think his story had such a powerful effect on British readers, when the British army seemed to be losing their first battle in the war? Also, why did so many people want to share 'The bowmen' with others or write their own version? List some possible reasons as follows: 'I think "The bowmen" was important for British readers in September 1914 because…'

Personal and Social Education/Circle Time: Trusting others

Age 5–11: Who do you trust?

For this activity, you will need a pet-carrier or an empty box with a few air-holes in the lid and a cuddly toy inside.

Tell the story of 'A whisper of wings', then produce the box. Say that you've brought in something to show… but it's a bit shy and it likes to stay in the dark, so you can raise the lid only a bit. Would anyone like to stroke it? (Don't say what it is.) Ask for a willing volunteer to do this without looking inside. Ask afterwards what they thought was inside, and why they trusted you.

Trust is very important. All the time, we trust different people to be reliable and they trust us to be reliable too. (Draw or show a picture of a spider's web on the board.) Just like this web, we're all connected, with lots of invisible threads, called relationships. We trust different people to do different things. Ask, 'What would help you to know if someone could be trusted... to keep a secret/to play a good game of football/to handle money/to care for a pet/to look after a young child?' Ask them to discuss in pairs and then feed back. Comment that there are different 'levels' of trust, and that being trusted with the care of young children is the most important on that list. You need to be very trustworthy to be allowed to do it.

Ask, 'Who would you trust... to stop traffic while you cross the road/to teach you how to spell a word/to mend your car if you had one/to help if there was an emergency in your house/to make you better if you were sick/to talk about God?' Encourage pupils to draw themselves in the middle of a page, then draw or write nearby the names of the people they trust most and say what they trust them to do, with illustrations to show these things in action. Afterwards, feed back responses, and ask, if a child doesn't feel safe, what should they do. (Tell a responsible adult as soon as possible.)

THOUGHT FOR THE DAY

Another word for trust is 'faith'. In the Bible, someone said that faith is very important: it means knowing what you can't see. Ask the children to shut their eyes and imagine living in a place where they couldn't trust anyone, and then to think of all those people they do trust to care for them. Silently say thank you for those people.

Prayer

Father God, help me to be wise about whom I trust, and, as I grow up, help me to be the kind of person who can be trusted by others. Amen

Tooth and claw

*

— UNIT 4 —

Tooth and claw:
Vernon Kellogg discusses reasons
for fighting a war

Background for teachers

During the First World War, many Americans were concerned about
the fate of the Belgian people whose country had been invaded
by Imperial Germany. Vernon Kellogg headed the Commission for
the Relief of Belgium, which ran relief missions to hand out food
and medical supplies to refugees and other victims of the war. The
occupying German army allowed the missions in because they
couldn't feed the refugees themselves, and also because the USA
was 'neutral': the Americans weren't yet fighting in the war. This
changed in 1917, especially after Americans like Vernon started
talking about what they'd seen and heard in Belgium.

'Headquarters nights', Vernon's record of conversations with
German officers, was published in an American magazine and
persuaded many that the USA should join the fight against Imperial
Germany. Kellogg's writings particularly detailed the way that
German officers saw the war as an exercise in 'natural selection'. As
a biological scientist, Kellogg believed in Charles Darwin's theory
of evolution but he became increasingly outraged by the way it
was used to justify a country's war on its neighbours. However,
some Americans thought the problem was the idea of evolution
itself and, after the war, started campaigning for the teaching of
evolutionary theory to be banned in American schools. Kellogg
opposed them—and the controversy continues in the USA up to
the present day.

The following story is based on Vernon's conversations recorded in 'Headquarters nights'.

STORY RETELLING: TOOTH AND CLAW

'Mr Kellogg,' one German officer asked him over the dinner table, 'why do so many people in the world hate us?'

How do you answer a question like that? Vernon Kellogg had just spent a long day sorting out food parcels for the Belgian women who were patiently lining up behind a table in a town hall. There were few men: the war had taken most of them away, as soldiers, prisoners of war and workers, into Germany and Belgium. Now he was having to eat a meal with the soldiers responsible, and be polite about it, or the German soldiers would send him back to the USA and stop his work. Vernon's charity was based in the same building as the German Army Headquarters in Belgium, so when the officers held a special meal and invited him along, it was difficult to say 'no'. After the meal, as the wine was passed around and the soldiers relaxed, he listened to what they were saying, and it worried him. If they asked him questions, he would try to be honest.

'Sir, are you really asking me why so many people hate you? It's because you invaded their countries with your soldiers. Your cannon shells and Zeppelin bombs have blown up their houses, and you've taken their men away to work in your factories and mines. That's why!'

The soldier took a puff on his cigar and shrugged. 'But that's what a strong people should do with the ones they defeat! You're a scientist, aren't you? Science tells us that life is a struggle and that the strongest survive. In nature, it's the most powerful creatures that win, especially the ones who are best organised, like the ants and the bees. They work together for the good of the ant nest or hive, and the strongest survive. That is what life is all about, isn't it?'

'But people aren't ants!' Vernon replied. 'When they're born, ants can't choose what they're going to do. They just do it. People are different. We learn; we care for others; we're superior to the other animals because we have bigger brains and higher thoughts.'

Another officer chipped in. 'But that is why we Germans should win this war—because our country is better than anyone else's. Our music and writing and thinking are superior to all the others. We organise things better, we make things better, and we fight better. The world needs us to be in control, so that we can make everything in it work better. What's wrong with that? The best should be in charge!'

Vernon was puzzled. 'But… what about those families I was helping to feed today? Your war isn't making their world any better.'

The officer nodded. 'It's sad, but that's war. We do what we have to do.'

Vernon exploded. '*But you don't have to be doing it!*' The room went quiet. He was a foreigner in a strange land. Had he gone too far? 'Listen,' he said, trying to explain himself and not make a scene. 'Yes, I am a scientist. I study insects. I know nature can be cruel. In California, I saw a wasp capture and paralyse the larvae of other insects, bury them, then lay an egg on top, so that her own larvae would have something living to eat as they grew bigger. Yes, nature can be brutal—but people are different. We have a conscience. We can think things through, work things out. Every human being is different and special... and free!'

After an embarrassed silence, the soldiers went politely back to their own conversations. They just didn't understand him, and Vernon didn't understand them either. They were friendly to him as an American and they went to church on Sunday, but, deep down, these soldiers seemed to believe in something cold and hard and cruel. You *can't* talk about people as if they're just animals, thought Vernon. Every person has a separate soul touched by the Creator.

He thought hard as he sat back, listening to their talk about the war and the ways they should try to win it. Vernon didn't believe in war but any country that started treating people like animals had to be stopped, before the whole world ended up like one giant anthill. He had to tell the people back home what these soldiers were saying, before it was too late. He couldn't simply stand back and let them win.

Religious Education: Selfishness and compassion

Age 5–7: Wanting what isn't yours

Young children have a lot to learn when they first come to school, as they need to learn to put the needs of others first sometimes. Classroom challenges such as 'How many thank yous can you say this week?' or 'Try to give everyone a smile today' have an impact. Vernon Kellogg's story could be introduced by first sorting the class into two groups. One group pretend to be seated on the ground having a meal. The other group play hungry soldiers who march in and take the plates of food, then go off to eat it nearby. How would the 'victims' feel? How would the soldiers justify it? Are they wrong?

Use this discussion to talk about what being selfish means. Then you could dramatise Vernon's story appropriately, playing him yourself as he gives out some food to the victims, then goes to eat with the soldiers. The soldiers can ask him their questions and all can discuss the answers. Jesus told his friends to 'love your neighbour as you love yourself' (see below). What might he be saying to those soldiers?

Age 5–7: The good Samaritan

In the story, Vernon Kellogg is angry that the soldiers don't care for the people whose country they've invaded. In the Bible, Jesus was once asked to explain what he thought were the most important rules for life. Then a lawyer asked him a question: 'Who is my neighbour?' Jesus answered with a story now famous throughout the world. Read aloud the story of the good Samaritan from Luke 10:25–37. Afterwards, ask: 'Can you remember the question this story was answering?'

Do one or more of the following role-play exercises.

- After telling or acting out the story, ask pupils to work in small groups to dramatise what they think is the key scene in the story, as a 'freeze-frame'. After rehearsal time, each group should recreate their key scene while the teacher walks around, asking different 'characters' in the scene, 'Who are you?' and 'What are you thinking/feeling?'
- Create a conscience alley, where the story is repeated with either the lawyer (scribe) or the priest being faced by a wounded man lying in the road. A volunteer pupil plays the lawyer/priest, standing at one end of an 'alley' created by the rest of the class, standing in two facing lines. The lawyer/priest walks slowly along the alley, pausing to face each person on either side alternately. One side of the alley is trying to persuade him to stop and help the wounded man. The other is trying to persuade him not to. Each member of the lines should suggest

a reason why he should or shouldn't stop. Having reached the end of the alley, the lawyer/priest turns to deliver a verdict on whether they will or won't stop, based on the strength of the arguments presented.

Then 'hot-seat' the lawyer/priest. Some members of the class ask him questions and others suggest possible answers he might give. They could even come out to the seat and answer 'in character'.

After the role-play, explain that this classic story is asking the same question that was worrying Vernon at the meal table: why should someone care for people who are different? Why not just let them die? In Jesus' story, the only person who stopped to help was the Samaritan, the foreigner. Jesus told his listeners to do the same. For him, being different or foreign shouldn't cut someone off from being helped or stop them offering help to someone else in need.

Extension

What might happen if we treated people in the way that animals are sometimes treated? (Who might get picked on or bullied?)

For reinforcement, set the task of retelling the story as a cartoon storyboard with a maximum of eight 'frames', encouraging pupils to use simple pin-men to illustrate what's happening. Ask them to tick which is the key scene, and to add speech or thought bubbles to show what the different characters are thinking. Why do they think this is the key scene? What might happen if people thought or acted differently? Ask them to draw a 'Take 2' key scene, showing the alternative.

Age 8–11: The last judgment

Explain that, for Christians, treating people as if they are simply animals is wrong. During the season of Advent, a Bible passage describing the last judgment (Matthew 25:31–46) is often read out in church. Give out copies of the passage.

Ask pupils to read the passage with a partner, underlining or circling any difficult or unfamiliar words, then working out their meaning by using a dictionary.

Ask pupils to answer the following questions in complete sentences.

- Who are the sheep and the goats?
- What rewards and punishments are being handed down by the judge?
- Why does the judge come down hard on people who have not helped those in need?
- What do you think the message of this passage is?

Extension

What do you think Jesus, 'the judge', would be saying to those churchgoing soldiers in the story who were arguing with Vernon?

Literacy: Animals, nice and nasty... and Zeppelins

Age 5–7: All creatures great and small

With your pupils, list a range of about 15 wild creatures. Then discuss: 'What do we like about them, or not? Can we classify them as nice or nasty?' Display the headings and discuss which category each creature would go into, and why. Draw out how selective we can be in 'liking' some creatures but not others, when all have their own place in the natural order, be they herbivores or predators. How would an environment be affected if one of those creatures died out? How might it affect the others? Add 'human beings' to the list. How would we classify *them*?

Set the task of researching and creating lists of words describing a favourite wild animal; older children could write a report explaining why the animal is liked. Discuss with the class some of the ways in which we human beings are different from the other creatures (including the fact that we can make lists and have this discussion).

Age 8–11: Zeppelin raids

Here's another (adapted) extract from 'Headquarters nights', in which Vernon Kellogg describes a banquet attended by a member of the German royal family. 'My officer' is the one whose job it was to keep an eye on Vernon all the time.

The Duke and the Zeppelins

One evening we had a larger and more distinguished dinner group than usual. The Duke, a war veteran and very close to the Kaiser, had come by motor with a small staff from his headquarters. My officer was all of a flutter with the importance and excitement of the event. He coached all of us—orderlies, myself, and resident guests—as to our proper behaviour during the visit. This was to consist chiefly of much stiff standing up, repeated formal bows, and respectful silence. No one was to start anything on his own initiative. Only His Highness could start any conversations.

The Duke entered to find us a fixed row of effigies, hands on trouser-seams, eyes front, chins up, in the receiving-room. His Highness was a small bewhiskered gentleman, very abrupt and disconcerting in manner, but not at all stupid, and very ready to express his opinions on all subjects of war and church history, his hobby. As he surveyed the row of effigies his keen eye spotted the non-uniformed American, and he directed a questioning look toward Lord W, the host. My officer made a concise explanation of the situation, which the Duke acknowledged with a grunt of understanding and the sharp question, 'But does he speak German?'

Lord W hastened to declare, 'Like a native'—which is far from true. Another grunt of satisfaction, a critical stare of examination, and finally a direct phrase of formal recognition. I reserved any exhibition of my fluent German, and merely bowed. My officer gave me an expressive look of approval and found a later chance to congratulate me on my 'success'. I suppose not being ordered out of the room may be called success, under the circumstances.

At dinner the personally conducted conversation leaped suddenly from church history to Zeppelining. It was just after one of those earlier London raids, when the great city was practically defenceless, and the German newspapers had been full for several days of accounts of the enormous damage and losses of life achieved by the raid. As a matter of fact there were some horrors—not extensive but intensive horrors—women and babies in several houses, and a bus full of passengers in a by-street, sickeningly mangled and murdered.

'Zeppelining is stupid!' the Duke declared. 'The men who ordered it are fools!' The table was struck silent. A Duke close to the Kaiser might say such a thing, but no one else could. Zeppelining had been declared wise and good by the General Staff, so it must be wise and good. One of the barons tried to argue.

'But His Highness will recall,' said the Baron, 'the military advantage of Zeppelining: it keeps guns and gunners in England which might otherwise be sent to the battle-line, and then there's the blowing up of arms factories, and the—ah—the military advantage generally. One must not consider the—ah—other side of the matter. A few—ah—civilians don't matter. It's all about the military advantage.'

His Highness snorted audibly and visibly. 'That is, of course, all that one does take into consideration. It is precisely because there is no military advantage in Zeppelining that it is stupid and the men who order it are stupid pigs. We don't blow up any arms factories, and for every miserable woman killed, hundreds and thousands of Englishmen rush into the army to come over to the front and fight us. We are doing their recruiting for them.' He fixed the squirming Baron with a cold grey eye. 'We are all only thinking of the military advantage. I repeat: Zeppelining is bad, and it is bad simply and entirely because it has no military advantage.'

That ended Zeppelining for the moment, until the very next subject introduced was the attitude of the neutral world, America in particular, toward Germany. The Baron suddenly turned to me. 'Why is there this universal hate of Germany? Why do you Americans hate us?'

It was too soon after what I had just heard. I blurted out, 'For things like the military advantage of Zeppelining.'

GLOSSARY

- Civilians: people who aren't in the armed forces
- Effigies: wax dummies that look like people
- Kaiser: the king of Germany
- Military advantage: whatever helps you win a war
- Neutral world: countries not fighting in the war
- Recruiting: encouraging people to join the armed forces
- War veteran: an important old soldier
- Zeppelins: powered airships, used for bombing cities

First, act out the introduction scene, to help your pupils feel the emotions involved in the reception room. After a warm-up of walking around the room like very stiff soldiers, greeting each other with a formal nod and keeping your distance, give out roles: the Duke, his staff and to the rest of the group, officers waiting in a line. Everybody must be standing stiffly to attention ('Attention!') as the Duke enters the room, his officers, lined up for inspection, bowing as he walks past. His staff should introduce each member of the line with a 'Sergeant this' or 'Commander that'. Everyone must act slightly frightened of doing or saying the wrong thing.

Reading comprehension

- What clues are there in the text that this is a very formal occasion?
- As Vernon describes the scene, are there any clues that tell you what he really thinks of the soldiers?
- In describing what people say, Vernon doesn't just use the word 'said'. List the other words and phrases he uses that show how someone might speak. Having made your list, choose one and use it in a new sentence.
- Summarise the scene in the reception room, using about 50 words, from either Vernon's point of view or that of the Duke.
- Do you agree with the Duke that the Zeppelin raids on London were stupid? Why? Is it always wrong to drop bombs on cities whose people aren't soldiers if you want to win a war? Discuss this with a partner, then write down your answer.

Science and RE: Asking big questions

Age 5–7: Nature 'red in tooth and claw'?

Vernon Kellogg wrote many books explaining science for the general public. *Insect Stories* is his collection of highly readable observations explaining life in the insect world. It can be downloaded free at www.gutenberg.org/files/39206/39206-h/39206-h.htm.

Read 'A narrow-waisted mother', the first chapter, which details in pupil-friendly language the lifecycle of the parasitic wasp mentioned in the 'Tooth and claw' story. Younger children could act out the story, using two hands as puppets for the wasp and the prey. Older pupils could retell it in diagrams. Fold a piece of paper into eight rectangles to provide the basic 'frames'. Use the first frame for the title. Afterwards, discuss whether nature is 'brutal' or 'unkind'. If it is, does that mean it's all right for people to be brutal or unkind as well? Why or why not?

Age 8–11: Arguments about natural selection and survival

Vernon Kellogg discovered that arguments about human beings and nature can lead in many directions. Here are three 'big idea' questions to develop with your class in discussion and creative writing. Each could be used as a basis for a discursive essay giving reasons for and against a point of view, with the chance to give a final considered opinion in the conclusion. This could be done in the context of the original, highly influential biblical creation story that sees God placing the human race in charge of the planet:

God said, 'Now we will make humans, and they will be like us. We will let them rule the fish, the birds, and all other living creatures.' So God created humans to be like himself; he made men and women. God gave them his blessing and said: 'Have a lot of children! Fill the earth with people and bring it under your control. Rule over the fish in the sea, the birds in the sky, and every animal on the earth.' (Genesis 1:26–28)

- Should we try to protect animal species that are in danger of extinction? Nowadays, many species of animal life are threatened with extinction because of human activity. In the UK, our native red squirrels are threatened by invading grey squirrels introduced from North America, which are larger, produce babies more quickly, and carry a disease that is lethal to reds but doesn't hurt the greys. Natural selection would say that it's fine for the reds to become extinct, but many British people want to protect the reds, creating special conservation areas where reds are encouraged to breed and greys are hunted down. Should they bother? Why or why not? Should humans intervene in 'natural processes' to protect endangered species such as red squirrels, pandas, blue whales and manatees, or less cuddly creatures such as the blue-fin tuna or the ladybird spider? If they're going to die out anyway, then what's the problem? List some arguments for and against preserving red squirrels or another species, researching some background information from a charity such as the World Wildlife Fund.

- The biologist Charles Darwin couldn't imagine how a kind God might choose to create a creature like the parasitic wasp described in the 'Tooth and claw' story (see www.darwinproject.ac.uk/entry-2814). What do you think?
- 'The way we treat animals affects the way we treat other people.' Do you agree? How might learning to care for a pet help someone to learn about caring for a person?

History: Propaganda

Every nation used propaganda posters to encourage popular support of the war effort. Studying them can give a flavour of the emotional buttons that were being pressed. The examples suggested here avoid too many of the stereotypes but should still be discussed with care and sensitivity.

Age 5–7: Studying propaganda from the First World War

Zeppelins were powered, rigid airships, originally used to carry cargo and passengers but used in war time for reconnaissance missions and the dropping of bombs. The German Zeppelin raids on London and other cities were the first air raids ever experienced in Britain, causing a great deal of panic, as the Germans intended. To begin with, there was no way of stopping them until a method was found to make RAF fighter planes that could fly higher, to fire newly invented incendiary bullets ('tracers') that set light to the hydrogen balloons keeping the Zeppelins aloft. What would it feel like to see one flying overhead?

Study these British propaganda posters:

- http://rememberwhen.gazettelive.co.uk/Rememberscarborough. jpg
- www.spartacus.schoolnet.co.uk/FWWzeppelinT.JPG
- http://watermarked.heritage-images.com/2490575.jpg

What were they saying about the Zeppelin raids? What were they trying to persuade people to feel and do? Do you think they were right? Design your own poster, telling British people what to do if they saw a Zeppelin in the sky. (Tell someone else? Take shelter?)

Age 8–11: Studying propaganda from the First World War

Before going to Belgium, Vernon Kellogg was a pacifist, opposing every use of armed force to solve international problems. His time with the German army in Belgium changed that view, and his book was used to encourage Americans to support the war against Germany. The First World War lasted from 1914 to 1918, and the USA came in on the 'Allied' side of Britain and France in April 1917, decisively giving the advantage to the Allies so that Germany finally lost. Study these American propaganda posters:

- http://blog.chron.com/txpotomac/files/legacy/wwi5.jpg
- http://rlv.zcache.com/the_kaiser_is_canned_vintage_world_war_1_poster-rff482730acac40979a4cb8cdbe679a7c_az8xt_400.jpg
- http://images.fineartamerica.com/images-medium-large/world-war-i-recruitment-poster-poster-everett.jpg
- http://en.wikipedia.org/wiki/File:Liberty-shall-not-perish-Pennell.jpeg

What were they trying to persuade people to feel and do? Do you think they were right? Design your own poster, telling American people how to support the war. (Buy Liberty Bonds, enlist in the Armed Forces, don't waste food, and so on. A Liberty Bond was a personal loan to the government, to be repaid with interest after the war.)

Personal and Social Education/Citizenship/ Circle Time: Caring is about not being selfish

Age 5–11: Thinking about life in a caring school

In pairs, find out three things about your partner that make them 'special'. Participants then have to explain (or, even better, mime) these special features to everyone else as a class. Ask, 'Who liked talking about themselves?' (Hands up.) 'Who found it harder to explain about their partner?'

Explain that this is normal. We are all experts on our own lives, and we know less about other people. We like people to care for us, but this can sometimes make us selfish: we want people to show care for us, without us having to care for them. Babies are naturally selfish: they just want someone to love them and care for them. Growing up is about learning not to be selfish, and that's sometimes very hard.

Why do you think we should care for others? Imagine coming to a school where everybody was completely selfish. What would it be like? What would people do and say? Set pupils the task of working in pairs, planning a 30-second play about life in a selfish school. (There will only be time for each actor to say and do one thing.) Afterwards, share performances, with the comment that life in a completely selfish school would be impossible. Discuss how a 'caring' school would be different. Ask pupils to replay their performances to show what life would be like if those people were being caring, not selfish. Demonstrate a few. Say that people can choose to live in different ways. Being selfish is easy, but it spoils things for everybody. Instead, we can choose to show care for others. It's much better!

Plenary discussion question

Terry Pratchett wrote in his book *Carpe Jugulum*, 'Sin is what you get when you start treating people like things, and things like people.' Do you agree? Can you think of any examples of what he means in any of the stories in this unit?

THOUGHT FOR THE DAY

Jesus told his followers to 'care for other people as you care for yourself'. This school can only be a truly happy school if everybody cares for each other like that.

Prayer

Father God, help me to show care for other people here, even when I don't feel like it. Help us all to make this a happy school. Amen

Tommy's zoo

— UNIT 5 —

Tommy's zoo:
Tom Bennett finds a new pet

Background for teachers

One key difference between the armies of the First World War and modern fighting formations was the former's reliance on animals. Michael Morpurgo's story *War Horse* illustrates perfectly the way all sides used horses in a variety of (often brutal) ways, but other creatures featured too, as foodstuffs (cattle, sheep, poultry), parasites (lice), scavengers (rats, mice, crows), pets and mascots (dogs, cats, goats, and even a lion in the story that follows), but also as a welcome distraction from the war. In their diaries or letters home, many soldiers mentioned their surprise at the beauty of the natural world. Not all of the Western Front was a sea of mud, especially at the beginning, and many soldiers found the presence of wild animals deeply affecting, as long as they weren't trying to steal their food or eat their boots.

The widespread keeping of pets in the trenches is particularly remarkable. Was this a desire to maintain sanity by nurturing something innocent? Along the front lines, many soldiers 'adopted' stray animals—usually dogs or cats, but there were others, as the story below describes.

STORY RETELLING: TOMMY'S ZOO

Imagine a phone conversation between two British officers on the Western Front (in Belgium and France) in the summer of 1916. One officer is Lieutenant-General George Fowke, who is Adjutant General, second-in-command of the British Army. He's very important. The other officer is Major-General 'Tom' Bridges, commanding 19th Western Division. We don't know if this conversation happened in exactly these words, but something like it definitely did.

Fowke: Hello, this is Lieutenant-General Fowke calling. Is that Major-General Bridges?

Bridges: It is, sir. I can hear you loud and clear.

Fowke: Good. I've just received a visit in my office from Mr Herbert Asquith. He used to be our Prime Minister.

Bridges: Yes, sir. I do remember that.

Fowke: He has been visiting our troops along the line, and he tells me that he came to have a look at your command post yesterday. Is that right?

Bridges: Yes, sir. I remember him clearly.

Fowke: Mr Asquith is a very important man in the government back home, so we always try to look our best when he visits us, don't we?

Bridges: Yes, we do, sir.

Fowke: We don't want the people back home thinking we're not taking this war seriously, do we?

Bridges: No, we don't, sir.

Fowke: So, Major-General, would you kindly explain to me why, when he was visiting your command post yesterday, Mr Asquith claims that he saw a lion?

Bridges: *(Silence.)* That was Poilu, sir.

Fowke: Poilu?

Bridges: He's my pet, sir. He's called Poilu because he's French. It means 'Shaggy'.

Fowke: So you have a pet lion, and you keep him with you at your command post?

Bridges: Yes, sir.

Fowke: We're talking about a real live lion, aren't we, with a mane and teeth, the sort of creature that normally lives in Africa?

Bridges: Yes, sir. In East Africa, the Serengeti. But he hasn't grown his mane yet. He's not old enough.

Fowke: *Major-General! I don't care a fig whether he's got a mane or not! Why have we got him with us in Belgium?*

Bridges: He was a present from a friend, sir.

Fowke: *A friend?*

Bridges: Well, sir, my friend Arthur was on leave in Paris and won a lion cub in a raffle. He didn't know what to do with him afterwards, so he gave him to me. I brought the lion cub back in a picnic hamper when I came off leave. He's been with us for over a year. He amuses the men. I tell them that when Poilu's big enough, he can come into battle with us. We feed him on dead horses, sir. He's no trouble.

Fowke: *Major-General! We're meant to be fighting a war, not keeping a zoo! Mr Asquith was not happy! Get rid of the lion!*

Bridges: But there's a problem with that, sir.

Fowke: What?

Bridges: Poilu doesn't want to go home. He likes being with us now. You can send someone to fetch Poilu, but he won't be happy if you try to take him away. And you wouldn't want to make him angry.

Fowke: Why not?

Bridges: Well, sir… because… he's a lion! But, sir, if you're going to make a fuss about us keeping a lion, then you'll need to be having a word with the Canadian soldiers too.

Fowke: Why?

Bridges: Because… *they've* got a bear!

* * *

Explain that Poilu the lion stayed with Tom Bridges on the front line for over a year, until Tom was injured and taken back to England. Poilu was brought back with another officer, although he scared a few people when he escaped from his crate on the ship during a storm at sea. The crew and passengers had to hide on the ship's bridge or up in the rigging until the officer had lured him into a first-class cabin and shut the door—from the outside.

Tom had been badly injured in the war and had to have a leg amputated. Afterwards, he said, 'I hope they gave it to the lion!' Poilu finally ended up in a private zoo, where he stayed for the rest of his life.

Religious Education: Lions and birds

Age 5–7: A lion in the classroom

Discuss what we know about lions. What would we need to think about if we wanted to keep a lion as a pet? Suppose we kept one in the cupboard over there: what would it need from us? How would you feel if it was your turn to feed it? Act this out in role-play, including the nervousness of getting closer, the feeding, and the relief of walking away afterwards. Discuss similar things that we may have been frightened of in the past, such as meeting a dangerous dog. What other real things might the soldiers have been frightened of as they went into battle?

Discuss the different reasons there might be for keeping a lion as a pet. (Poilu came initially as a small cub in a picnic basket.) What might it feel like if we could touch it, stroke it, even carry it? When the lion was grown up, how big would it be? How would it move? Act out prowling around the room like a lion, growling and roaring. How do you think the soldiers felt about having a lion as their pet? (Proud? Brave? Powerful?) How would they have talked about it to others? Discuss how keeping a lion may have been a symbol for the soldiers—a kind of badge to show how brave they were.

Other animals were kept as regimental mascots too, including bears, monkeys, goats and even geese. What do we think keeping a pet can do for someone who's feeling lonely or stressed?

Mention the Bible story of the first man giving names to all the animals in Genesis 2:19–20. Although we are more intelligent than the other animals, why do we think we should name them and care about them? Discuss what valuable lessons might be found in keeping a pet. What might animals have to teach us about the God who created them? This could become a thoughtful writing task.

Age 5–7: Birdwatching on the battlefield

Many soldiers in the trenches were fascinated by the wild birds that flew overhead or scavenged for food nearby. During a normal day, the natural world could provide a fascinating distraction, especially when there was frequently nothing to do but stand guard and keep watch. The birds didn't seem to be worried, did they? They just got on with looking for food whenever they wanted, and if they were scared, they could just fly away. Lucky birds!

Ask the children if they worry about things sometimes. (Don't start a classroom discussion: this needs to be unpacked carefully and sensitively.) Explain that everybody worries about things sometimes. If you can, reminisce about a worry you used to have as a child. (Fischy Music have an excellent song available for download and on CD called 'Bag of worries', to the tune of 'Drunken Sailor': see www.fischy.com/downloads/music-clips.)

Explain that the soldiers of the First World War had a great many things to worry about. What do the pupils think these were? (List them together on a 'worry bag' diagram.) Being frightened isn't new. Sometimes people have found the Bible helpful when they're feeling helpless. Many of the wistful comments found in soldiers' letters and diaries consciously use words and phrases from the Bible. Read Jesus' comments about worry and birds (Matthew 6:25–27), and the sending out of the disciples (Matthew 10:29–31).

If you could sum up what Jesus is saying here in seven words or fewer, what would it be? Explain that there is a difference between being worried about something you can't change (for example, how tall you are) and something you can change (for example, if you feel you're being bullied and need to tell someone). Emphasise, in line with school policy, that if any child is really worried about something, they should tell a responsible adult. Then set the task of drawing the face of someone who is worried, adding what they're thinking in thought bubbles nearby, as words or a picture. Draw some birds around the face, and copy out what you think Jesus' words might be saying to this person. Write some of these positive messages on stencilled outlines of birds to create a wall display.

Age 8–11: Animals as symbols

Keeping a pet could be a welcome distraction from the horrors of war. Extend the 'Lion in the classroom' activity for younger children by developing the discussion about what it might mean to the soldiers. A mascot could become a symbol of:

- Strength: healthy animals have a natural grace and power that we can admire.
- Youth: a young animal has a spontaneous interest in its surroundings that can be fascinating to watch.
- Community: a mascot becomes a focal point of shared interest and responsibility for a group. Many soldiers shared their own food with their pets or went foraging to be able to feed them.

- Good humour: see the Literacy activity on page 89 about the two geese.
- Innocence: animal minds are less complicated than those of human beings, with simpler desires and needs that are more easily met.
- Home: see the chaplain's quote in the Personal and Social Education activity on page 91.

Which creature would your pupils like to adopt as a personal or class symbol, and why? What qualities does it have that we would want to emulate? This idea could be extended into further work on signs and symbols, using lions or other images from the natural world, and including biblical imagery such as the 'Lion of Judah' (Genesis 49:9). Modern synagogues often use the imagery of two lions facing each other with the Torah in the middle, as if they are protecting it. The author of Mark's Gospel is often represented as a lion. 'The Chronicles of Narnia' by C.S. Lewis also feature Aslan the lion—a character commonly thought to symbolise Jesus Christ.

Age 8–11: Psalm 55: For the wings of a dove

Ask the class to discuss a time when they remember being frightened. What happened? What did they want to do? Explain that in the First World War, many soldiers were terrified of being killed or badly wounded in battle. Sometimes, the words of the Bible were a help to them, especially the Psalms, many of which were written long ago by David, another brave soldier. Psalm 55 speaks of the terror of dying, and the desire to escape on 'the wings of a dove' (vv. 1–8). Display the passage, and read it together.

Say that wanting to escape from danger is natural. Some people try to escape their problems by distracting themselves—thinking of something else, or using food or alcohol or other things to make themselves feel better for a while. Similarly, some TV programmes or films are called 'escapist' because they're fun but have nothing to do with real life. People can run away from their problems but it usually gets them into worse trouble. (This might be a good time to mention the dangers of running away from home.)

Later in the psalm, David says, 'Cast your cares on the Lord and he will sustain you' (v. 22, NIV). He doesn't run away, but he does ask for help. Discuss with the class: 'Who can we take our worries to instead of trying to avoid them?' List the kinds of 'helpers' available to us. Set the task of drawing a soldier in his trench, with a 'bag of worries' beside him. What might be in there? Nearby, copy out a section of the psalm that might be helpful to him.

Age 5–11

In plenary, you could play a sung musical setting of Felix Mendelssohn's famous 'Oh, for the wings of a dove', which is based on this Bible passage.

Literacy: Fascinating animals

Age 5–7: Animal haiku

Many primary classrooms use images of animals to enhance a general display. How many can your pupils spot? List them together, then ask why we use images of animals. Brainstorm a list of adjectives that we could use to describe animals.

Then introduce the class to haiku poems: the Japanese way of writing poetry in verses of three lines, with five syllables for the first line, seven for the middle and five for the last. Set children the challenge of choosing one animal, then conveying its true nature in a haiku. The name of the creature must feature only in the title.

Afterwards, discuss, 'Did we choose animals that have some feature we'd like to have?'

Age 8–11: Creating a script

'Tommy's zoo' is an imagined conversation based on a soldier's reminiscence found in the book *Tommy's Ark* by Richard van Emden (Bloomsbury, 2010). What are the key features of a script? Create a new script based on a similar situation. A Battery, 52nd Brigade (Royal Field Artillery) had two geese named Jimmy and Jane. They were originally purchased for Christmas lunch in 1915, but their personalities won over the soldiers so much that they were kept as mascots, survived the war and ended up in a zoo. The decision to spare their lives was taken at a spoof court-martial with speeches from the 'prosecution' and the 'defence', with a jury to vote on the outcome. For a simpler alternative, 48th Battalion (Canadian Scottish) kept a grizzly bear.

Music

Age 8–11: Dramatising the war horse

For centuries, horses were used in battle, being replaced by motorised vehicles only in the last century. Job 39:19–25 is a passage about a war horse from one of the oldest poetic books of the Bible, which is a long series of arguments about why people suffer. Towards the end of the book, Job asks God why his life has known so much pain, and 'out of the storm' God answers (chs. 38—41) by showing him all the things he's created in the natural world. Entranced, Job is silenced. God's 'answer' details a range of remarkable creatures, at least one (the dragonish Leviathan) mythical, but the passage about a war horse is a striking piece of description in itself. Share it with your class in at least two versions, one being the King James Version.

Then divide the class into groups to set this passage to music to make a dramatic reading, challenging them to use drumbeats to convey the marching of soldiers, coconut shells (or similar) for the sound of horses' hooves, and so on. Give them copies of both Bible versions, allowing them to choose their preferred version, highlighting words and phrases for illustration with different sounds. At least one child in each group should be given the task of reading the script aloud. Encourage them to provide a range of 'background' and 'foreground' sounds.

If appropriate to the age and maturity of the class, show them a section from a war film that uses music to enhance the depiction of a cavalry charge, such as *War Horse* (Stephen Spielberg, 2011) or *Henry the Fifth* (Laurence Olivier, 1944), with particular reference to the use of music, showing the extract with and without the soundtrack.

History: Studying contemporary accounts

Age 7–11: Looking at original source material

Tommy's Ark is a fascinating collection of first-hand accounts of the lives of soldiers and animals in the First World War (including Tom Bridges' story about his pet lion) and is well worth buying for both general interest and classroom source material. When using original source material (text or images) with pupils, use the following prompts:

- We notice…
- It made us wonder…
- We also want to ask…
- What does this original source material reveal to us about life in the past?

Personal and Social Education/Circle Time: Caring for animals

Age 5–11: Caring for pets

One crucial difference between human beings and the other creatures that populate this planet is that the lives of animals are defined by their environment. By contrast, human beings try to shape their environment, constantly adapting it for their own comfort and well-being by building shelters and homes, developing increasingly efficient ways to source food, and domesticating animals for a range of purposes, which includes the keeping of pets for company.

Ask your class which of them has a pet. Ask volunteers to describe what they have to do to look after the pet. Do they take a share of the responsibilities?

Show pictures (from Google Images) of soldiers from the First World War with their pets. Many of the soldiers had to go without food themselves to ensure that their pet had enough. Why do you think they bothered? One chaplain in the trenches saw a kitten that had been kept in a soldier's dugout (shelter) and was now hiding in a bomb crater. He wrote:

If anything speaks of home it is a kitten. It carries our mind back to the blazing fire and the cat sleeping within the fender. Yet here are thousands of lads who have not been home for months, and here are poor dugouts—the crudest imitations of homes—that have been battered in. Day and night these soldiers dream of home. In a trench, a man is as out of place as a kitten is in a crate, and as surely will he leave the trench for the fireside. The crater belongs to war, the kitten to peace. The one speaks of death, the other of life.

TOMMY'S ARK, P. 153

THOUGHT FOR THE DAY

Ask every child to close their eyes and picture a pet they care for now, or might want to have one day. What is it that we like about our pets?

Prayer

Father God, thank you for the animals we love and are responsible for. Remind us when we forget to give them all the care they need, because they rely on us for their lives and comfort. Amen

A hurricane of poetry

*

— UNIT 6 —

A hurricane of poetry: Fred Roberts gives soldiers a voice in *The Wipers Times*

Background for teachers

The Wipers Times was a 'trench newspaper' created by soldiers on the front line from February 1916 to December 1918. As 12th Battalion Sherwood Foresters were helping to defend the Belgian town of Ypres from a German attack, an abandoned printing press was discovered in pieces by Captain F.J. 'Fred' Roberts. After another soldier (who was a printer in civilian life) got the press working again, Roberts decided to edit and publish his own newspaper with anyone who cared to help. They had plenty of paper and ink, but no text. 'None of us were writing men,' he said later. 'We just wrote down any old thing that came into our heads. Little incidents of daily life were turned into adverts or small paragraphs.' The first edition (100 copies) sold out almost immediately, as did the second (200 copies). When the press was destroyed by enemy shelling, Roberts found another. When the division eventually moved on, so did the newspaper, changing its name each time as more editions were produced with larger print runs (up to 1,000 copies), usually at monthly intervals—all while its many contributors were getting on with the bloody and soul-destroying business of fighting a war.

How did they manage to do it, and why? Perhaps, when facing the prospect of violent death in the worst possible living conditions, there was a refuge in simply being creative. These soldiers were reminding themselves what made them human, celebrating it and keeping themselves sane. Whether you believe in a Creator or not, creativity matters.

The conversation below is fictional, but the setting and events are real.

STORY RETELLING: A HURRICANE OF POETRY

There was a whizzing sound overhead, and a loud bang. Then the shell exploded in a hail of hot metal splinters. Everyone dived for cover again. The Germans had been shelling the British trenches all day, so the Sherwood Foresters were busily repairing them, digging out spadeful after spadeful of cold, wet, stinking mud, then fixing planks into the trench walls to firm them up and putting down duck-boards to keep feet dry. Every few minutes there'd be another 'whizz!' and everyone would drop down in the mud. Whizz! Bang! Splat! Already today, three men had been hit by shell splinters and sent back to the field hospital. It was difficult work, but nobody had been killed—not yet. But they found some pretty awful things in their digging—sometimes the body of a soldier killed in a previous battle. Captain Roberts' men were getting tired, and tired people can make dangerous mistakes. (Last night, an officer had nearly drowned, slipping into a muddy shell-hole full of water. That's why they were repairing the trench today.)

'Everybody stop for ten minutes!' shouted Captain Roberts. The Sherwood Foresters downed tools and retreated into their dugouts for a quick cigarette and brew-up while someone kept watch at the parapet. Once under cover, the captain removed his satchel and started leafing through some papers. Whizz, bang! Another shell crashed overhead.

'Oh no, not more,' he muttered. 'Can't we do any better than this? Somebody *make it stop*!'

'More what, sir?' asked his sergeant, sitting nearby. 'Are you all right, sir? Is it the shelling?'

'No, sergeant, it's all this stupid *poetry*! I can't stand it any more!'

'The poetry, sir?' The sergeant looked baffled. The captain held up his sheets of paper, grinning.

'Sergeant, I'm trying to run a newspaper, and I've asked the men to write me something interesting to put in it, but look at the rubbish they keep sending me.' He handed over some handwritten sheets. 'I want them to send me jokes and stories, and look what happens. Poems, poems and more poems! This is the latest lot. Look at them. Poems about being shot at, poems about rats, poems about girlfriends back home. It just won't stop.'

The sergeant flicked through the sheets, then stopped and read one quietly.

'This one's not bad, sir. "To my chum." Listen to this.

'We've weathered the storm two winters long
We've managed to grin when all went wrong
Because together we fought and fed
Our hearts were light; but now—you're dead.'

He handed it back. The captain read the whole poem through, and frowned. 'It's not going to cheer anybody up, is it? Do you think a poem about a dead friend should go in our newspaper?'

'Yes, sir.'

'Why?'

'It's personal, sir,' said the sergeant. 'It's about his friend. He's saying what he feels, and that's not a bad thing. It's not Shakespeare, but if it was me as editor, I'd put it in. If you don't, then who else is going to print it?'

The ten minutes were up and the Sherwood Foresters went

back to repairing the trench as more whizz-bangs came flying overhead. As they shovelled more mud, and found another body that would need to be reburied, Captain Roberts thought about the sergeant's words. Yes, the poem had to be printed in his newspaper. Friends needed to be remembered, and *The Wipers Times* would be the place to do it.

Religious Education: Finding a voice

Morale is crucial for any army, and *The Wipers Times* kept spirits up by sharing idle gossip and in-jokes while allowing soldiers to have a gentle moan at their lot. Friendship counts when people are under stress, and the *Times* enabled servicemen to share their burdens with each other in print.

Age 5–7: Powerful words

Share a few silly jokes appropriate to the age group, then ask what makes the jokes funny. Why do we like to hear them? Explain that words can be very powerful and make us feel good inside. Together, let's name and list as many different feelings as we can, using the song 'If you're happy and you know it, clap your hands' and adding different emotions and responses. Say that words can encourage people and calm people's fears, as in the story of Jesus calming the storm (Mark 4:35–41). We can tell stories that make people feel good, and that's how so many traditional stories probably started—with friends telling them to each other.

The Bible is full of encouraging words, such as Psalm 46. Share a few extracts from the psalm. Which words or phrases would be most helpful to frightened soldiers? List them on a display, then set pupils the task of copying and illustrating three favourites. Challenge them to say something encouraging to as many people as possible this week.

Age 5–7: Friendship

What is friendship? What makes someone a good friend? In the Bible, there are many stories of friendships that stood the test of time—and a few that didn't. This article from the Barnabas website has some useful ideas for exploring the theme of friendship with young children, including the creation of a classroom display: www.barnabasinschools.org.uk/exploring-values-with-the-bible-friendship/.

Age 8–11: Finding a voice

The Wipers Times gave soldiers (many of them teenagers) a place to express themselves in print for the first time. In the Bible, God gave a young man called Jeremiah the responsibility of speaking the truth to anyone who would listen, at a time when his nation was falling apart. Understandably, this frightened Jeremiah, but he was encouraged with a special message. Share with pupils the dialogue from Jeremiah 1:4–10.

Afterwards, set pupils the task of discussing and answering these questions:

- Jeremiah said to God, 'I do not know how to speak; I am only a child' (v. 6, NIV). Which part of God's answer do you think gave him the most courage to speak out?
- 'I have put my words in your mouth. See, today I appoint you over nations and kingdoms to uproot and tear down, to destroy and overthrow, to build and to plant' (vv. 9–10, NIV). How can words do this? Suggest ways in which someone's words can change the world.
- What are the most powerful words that have ever been said to you?

Extension

What message would you like the whole world to hear? How could you use jokes and humour to share that message?

Literacy: War poetry

As Captain Roberts discovered, writing poetry was a popular activity for many soldiers in the First World War, and some of their work is still remembered and studied today. However, in a *Wipers Times* editorial (20 March 1916), Roberts wrote:

We regret to announce that an insidious disease is affecting the Division, and the result is a hurricane of poetry. Subalterns have been seen with a note-book in one hand, and bombs in the other, absently walking near the wire in communion with the muse… The Editor would be obliged if a few of the poets would break into prose as a paper cannot live by 'poems' alone.

Much of the war poetry studied in schools today conveys the cynicism of survivors who felt that their comrades' sacrifice had been forgotten by their country, but *The Wipers Times* displays another side.

Age 5–7: *The Wipers Times* verse

A soldier wrote this poem about his pet dog, who was rather good at catching rats, and had it published in *The Wipers Times* of 8 September 1917.

Jim

A hard little, scarred little terrier,
With a touch of the sheep-dog thrown in—
A mongrel—no matter

There's no better ratter
In trenches or billet, than Jim.

A tough little, rough little beggar;
And merry, the eyes of him.
But no Tartar or Turk
Can do dirtier work
With an enemy rat, than Jim.

And when the light's done, and night's falling,
And the shadows are darkling and dim,
In my coat you will nuzzle
Your pink little muzzle
And growl in your dreams, little Jim.

Discuss the rhyming scheme (which is the same as a limerick) and the adjectives that describe Jim. Why do you think this soldier is keeping him as a pet? What does the last verse tell you about his feelings for Jim?

Age 8–11: War poetry from *The Wipers Times*

Here's a spoof of Rudyard Kipling's famous poem 'If', which reveals quite a lot about life in the trenches. After noting examples of the precise rhyming scheme, pupils could list some of the things in a soldier's life that it complains about. Which do they think are the three worst features, and why? Can they sum up what they think this poem is trying to say in 15 words or fewer?

If (1914–1918) With the usual apologies…

If you can drink the beer the Belgians sell you,
And pay the price they ask with ne'er a grouse,
If you believe the tales that some will tell you,
And live in mud with ground sheet for a house,

If you can live on bully and a biscuit,
And thank your stars that you've a tot of rum,
Dodge whizz-bangs with a grin, and as you risk it
Talk glibly of the pretty way they hum,

If you can flounder through a C.T. nightly
That's three-parts full of mud and filth and slime,
Bite back the oaths and keep your jaw shut tightly,
While inwardly you're cursing all the time,

If you can crawl through wire and crump-holes reeking
With feet of liquid mud, and keep your head
Turned always to the place which you are seeking,
Through dread of crying you will laugh instead,

If you can fight a week in Hell's own image,
And at the end just throw you down and grin,
When every bone you've got starts on a scrimmage,
And for a sleep you'd sell your soul within,

If you can clamber up with pick and shovel,
And turn your filthy crump-hole to a trench,
When all inside you makes you itch to grovel,
And all you've had to feed on is a stench,

If you can hang on just because you're thinking
You haven't got one chance in ten to live,
So you will see it through, no use in blinking,
And you're not going to take more than you give,

If you can grin at last when handing over,
And finish well what you had well begun,
And think a muddy ditch a bed of clover,
You'll be a soldier one day, then, my son.

GLOSSARY

- grouse: moan
- bully: tinned beef, part of army rations
- whizz-bangs: German high-speed artillery shells
- C.T.: communications trench
- oaths: bad language
- crump-hole: shell crater
- starts on a scrimmage: feels like breaking

'To my chum' is the poem in the story 'A hurricane of poetry', printed in *The Wipers Times* on 20 March 1916. It speaks of the sadness of losing a good friend in battle. We don't know the story behind it.

To my chum

No more we'll share the same old barn
The same old dug-out, same old yarn
No more a tin of bully share
Nor split our rum by a star-shell's glare
So long, old lad.

What times we've had, both good and bad
We've shared what shelter could be had
The same old crump-hole when the whizz-bangs shrieked
The same old billet that always leaked
And now—you've 'stopped one'.

We've weathered the storm two winters long
We've managed to grin when all went wrong
Because together we fought and fed
Our hearts were light; but now—you're dead
And I am Mateless.

Well, old lad, here's peace to you
And for me, well, there's my job to do
For you and the others who are at rest
Assured may be that we'll do our best
In vengeance.

Just one more cross by a strafed roadside
With its GRC, and a name for guide,
But it's only myself who has lost a friend,
And though I may fight through to the end,
No dug-out or billet will be the same,
All pals can only be pals in name,
But we'll all carry on till the end of the game
Because you lie there.

GLOSSARY

- barn: farm building
- dug-out: shelter in the side of a trench
- yarn: story
- a tin of bully: tinned beef, part of army rations
- split our rum: share their rum ration
- star-shell's glare: parachute flare used at night
- crump-hole: shell crater
- whizz-bangs: German high-speed artillery shells
- billet: place of shelter
- 'stopped one': been killed by a bullet
- strafed roadside: a road often hit by enemy fire
- GRC: Grave Registration Commission: a code number recording a burial place

Explain that this poem expresses a personal loss: a soldier is remembering his friend killed in battle. After an experience like this, many people can find it helpful to put their feelings down on paper as he did. Together, list the author's special memories of the friendship described here. Pupils should then be set the task of annotating a copy of the poem, highlighting unusual words or phrases and sharing ideas on what they might mean, with help from the teacher, and adding written or drawn explanations and further questions. Afterwards, pupils should copy out their favourite section of the poem, with a note explaining what impresses them most about it.

Extension

Teachers wanting to steer their pupils to other more respected war poets should try Siegfried Sassoon's poems 'A working party' (depicting life in the trenches, similar to the description in the story) and 'The General', which is shorter and more satirical.

History: Studying *The Wipers Times*

The Wipers Times provides a brilliant insight into the lives of soldiers in the First World War, especially the spoof advertisements that send up the daily absurdities of military life. Was it just their cheerfulness that kept the army going sometimes?

Age 8–11: Spoof adverts

What do the following spoof adverts from *The Wipers Times* tell us about the lives of soldiers in the trenches?

• Unwanted gifts: Many soldiers were sent gifts from home, but they weren't always very useful. This spoof advert lists the sorts of things no sensible soldier would want. Can you guess why? Write a letter home from a soldier who has just received this 'Xmas Box', explaining why he doesn't like it and saying what he really wants.

REMEMBER THE LADS IN THE TRENCHES!

YOU WANT TO GIVE YOUR BRAVE DEFENDERS WHAT THEY WANT!

YOU DON'T KNOW! WE DO!

Let us send a parcel for you. All you have to do is send us five, ten or twenty shillings, and the name and address of your soldier boy—WE DO THE REST.

Our ten shilling Xmas Box contains:

1 tin compressed beef
1 bottle lime juice
1 pyjama case
1 pair carpet slippers
1 umbrella
1 two-pound pot of jam (plum and apple)
and a nice souvenir from London—a piece of A.A. shrapnel

- Mad inventions: Nobody actually tried to invent something like this—did they? What would it have looked like? Make your own design with labels and diagrams to show how it might work.

IS YOUR FRIEND A SOLDIER?

DO YOU KNOW WHAT HE WANTS?

NO!! WE DO!!!

Send him one of our latest
IMPROVED PATTERN COMBINATION
UMBRELLA AND WIRE CUTTER

These useful appliances can be used simultaneously. No more colds caught cutting the wire. He will be delighted with it and will find a use for it.

PRICES—Gold Plated 500 fr. Silver Plated 39 fr.
Ordinary 15 fr.
With a shooting stick attachment 5 fr. extra.

SEND HIM ONE AT ONCE

- Duck-boards were the planks used to firm up a trench floor. They didn't always work. Does this advert celebrate something that really happened with the Royal Engineers? Write the script for a short play about a grumpy company commander who comes to inspect some soldiers in their trench, asking questions and telling them off… and then has 'an accident'.

To harrassed subalterns

Is your life miserable? Are you unhappy?
Do you hate your company commander?

YES! Then buy him one of our patent tip duck-boards
You get him on the end, the duck-board does the rest
Made in three sizes, and every time a 'Blighty'

'If once he steps on to the end
Twill take a month his face to mend'

WRITE AT ONCE & ENSURE HAPPINESS

Extension

Write a spoof *Wipers Times* advertisement for a British First World War tank. (They were slow, often broke down and, because the drivers couldn't always see where they were going, could be as dangerous to British soldiers as they were to the enemy.)

Citizenship: Comic relief?

Age 5–11: Charity fundraising

The publishers of *The Wipers Times* gave all their profits to charity. Many modern comedians get involved in charities by performing benefit gigs and by actively supporting their work. Could your school support a charity by putting on a fundraising show? (Warning: check all jokes beforehand…) Alternatively, consider creating a class magazine for charity, packed with funny stories and stupid jokes (which will be a lot easier to censor!).

Personal and Social Education/Circle Time: Keeping positive

Age 5–11: Seeing the big picture

The Wipers Times shows how being cheerful and creative made a difference for the soldiers who created and bought it. They shared jokes, told funny stories and tried to see the best in things. It's called having a positive mental attitude.

- Illustration 1: Show a glass of water, half full. Ask: 'Is this glass half full or half empty?' Discuss in pairs, then ask for responses and reasons why. Explain that sometimes we can easily slip into being a 'pessimist', only seeing the bad in everything and missing the good—or we can be an 'optimist', who does the opposite. That can seriously affect the way we live our lives.
- Illustration 2: Show two empty glasses. Turn one upside down, and balance a few marbles on its upturned base. Place an equal number of marbles in the second glass, which is the right way up. Ask: 'Which one is most likely to lose its marbles if you carry it around?' (The upturned one.) 'Why?' (It hasn't got raised sides to keep the marbles in.) Explain that people can be

like these two glasses. Some people go through life nervously, constantly worried that something bad is about to happen, but other people can be more secure—they're not so worried.

This is all to do with the way we see ourselves, and seeing the bigger picture. If you've had a bad experience, it can lead you into thinking that everything in life is bad and that more bad things will happen. But if you've had a bad experience, you can also try to work out what happened and make sense of it, asking other people what they think, talking about your fears but not being controlled by them. Telling funny stories can be part of that response, because, if you can learn to smile at your troubles, it can help them to go away.

It also helps to have a big picture of life that shows how we all fit into it. That's why so many people in the world have some kind of faith in a God who cares for them, because that picture says that whatever happens, I still matter to God and he won't forget me. So, are you a 'glass half full' or a 'glass half empty' person? Are you an optimist or a pessimist? It's all to do with your big picture!

What could you do today to cheer up someone who needs it? That's big-picture stuff. And remember, people can change their pictures.

THOUGHT FOR THE DAY

Put the two glasses in a place where everyone can see them. Ask the pupils to think of all the people who love and care for them and quietly say 'thank you' for them. Ask: 'Could you be one of the people helping someone else by being a good friend today?'

Prayer

Father God, thank you for loving me. When I'm finding life difficult, help me to remember how special I am to you. Amen

'Stretcher bearer!'

*

'Stretcher bearer!' William Coltman and Richard Tawney in No Man's Land

Background for teachers

Lance-Corporal William Coltman (1/6th battalion, 46th North Midland Division) was a member of the Plymouth Brethren. His Christian beliefs prevented him from taking up arms but he still volunteered in 1915 to 'do his bit', getting transferred to a front-line stretcher-bearing role straight after enlisting. (Volunteers got more choice about where they served.) He was a short man but incredibly strong and tough, and he specialised in carrying casualties quickly to safety on his back.

Paramedics today speak of the 'golden hour' (the first hour after a person has been injured), emphasising the need for fast emergency treatment of severe injuries, but First World War stretcher bearers like William Coltman already knew that a quick evacuation to hospital could make all the difference as to whether someone survived or not.

For his exploits in saving British (and German) lives on the battlefield, William received a string of medals, culminating in the Victoria Cross, despite never firing a shot. As the most decorated NCO (non-commissioned officer) of the war, William was present at the burial of the Unknown Soldier, when the coffin was brought to Westminster Abbey in 1920. Many years later, when talking about his experiences, he said, 'I don't believe in guns and war.'

The incident related here took place towards the end of the war, after the British had breached the Hindenberg Line (a series of German defences previously thought impregnable) and were successfully pushing forward towards German soil. Four weeks later, the Germans surrendered.

STORY RETELLING: 'STRETCHER BEARER!'

It was 4 October 1918. As machine-gun bullets zipped overhead, William took a quick peek round a tree. 'Stretcher bearer!' 'Stretcher bearer!' Wounded soldiers from his regiment were shouting from different places further up the hill. The battle of Beaurevoir was going badly for the British. Yesterday, they'd pushed the enemy back a long way but had had to stop near the top of Mannequin Hill. Now it was daylight and the Germans had brought up reinforcements, placing machine guns on high ground to the left and right, from where they could hit the British troops. As the Germans started firing, men started falling. The British quickly retreated down the hill to somewhere safer, but they'd left many wounded behind.

William shrugged and took a deep breath. He picked his moment, then dashed forward, racing up the slope, dipping into whatever cover he could find, scanning the ground around him for wounded soldiers who needed help. Over there! A soldier lay on his side, bleeding heavily, shot through the leg. William crawled forward and dragged him back into cover as more bullets pinged past.

'Bill! You found me!' groaned the soldier. 'They said you would!'

William was swiftly unrolling a bandage, eyes darting around for danger. 'Who's they?'

'The others. They said, "If anyone can find you if you cop it, it'll be Billy. He don't get lost!"'

The bandage was quickly tied around the leg, fixing a tight dressing to stop the bleeding. 'It's a bit hard to get lost today,' William grunted, 'what with them up there and us down here! Now, are you ready?'

'For what?' asked the soldier. 'Oh…', as William gave him a shot of pain-killing morphine.

'Listen, I'm going to carry you. You're safer back with a doctor than here.'

'Can't you stay with me?'

A sad shake of the head. 'There's others to get besides you, lad. Ready?'

William pulled the soldier into a sitting position, lifted him over his shoulder, got to his feet, and ran back down the valley, dodging from side to side as more bullets whipped up the long grass around them. After a long minute, he was sheltering behind the deep sides of a road, gently placing the man on a stretcher. Soon, the soldier would be taken back to base hospital by German prisoners. They were very helpful and seemed quite happy to have been captured.

Major Downing, the Commanding Officer, was watching. 'Did you see what that Lance-Corporal just did?' he remarked to a messenger. 'Unbelievable… And he's been doing that for three years.'

William made more rescues that day, and was awarded the Victoria Cross 'for most conspicuous bravery, initiative and devotion to duty… On three occasions [he] carried comrades on his back to safety, thus saving their lives. This very gallant NCO tended the wounded unceasingly for 48 hours.'

Religious Education: Shepherds and sheep

Age 5–7: The good shepherd

Having shared William's story, explain that there's a similar story told by Jesus of a shepherd and a lost sheep (Luke 15:1–7). Ask: 'How many ways can you think of in which sheep are similar to people?' After discussing the replies, highlight the key point in this parable—that both can get lost. Jesus said that people can get themselves into all sorts of trouble, but, as the good shepherd, he is there to help, as William was.

As a warm-up, play the party game 'Keeper of the keys' as 'Sheep rescue'. It's a good quietening game. Put a model or toy sheep under a chair. A child sits on the chair as the big bad wolf, blindfolded. The other children sit in a circle around the chair and silently put up their hands as volunteers to creep up and try to rescue the sheep. The child on the chair has three attempts to hear and point at the would-be rescuer.

Next, act out different feelings/sensations in the story (grumpy/ hungry/ naughty/running away/eating nice food/nervous/worried/ terrified/relieved/safe), making different 'faces' or statues at a given signal. Then tell the story in groups, acting out different parts as you go (the lost sheep, other sheep, wolves, lions, the shepherd).

Alternatively, a downloadable verse version is available online: visit www.barnabasinschools.org.uk/downloads/9781841012438_ reading1.mp3/.

One follow-up challenge activity is for groups to create a 'Where's my sheep?' fold-out storybook with flaps for younger children, similar to 'Where's Spot?' You might need first to agree on a basic script written together (using your classroom whiteboard), which can then be printed off and creatively illustrated. Different children in a group could work simultaneously on their different pages, which could then be glued together.

Age 8–11: Trusting God in the valley

Through the centuries, many soldiers have been inspired by the biblical poetry of another warrior—David, slayer of Goliath and king of Israel. His psalms speak of the highs and lows of being alive, living dangerously and trusting in the Lord God to see him through.

Psalm 23, written by David, is memorable for its reference to walking through 'the valley of the shadow of death'. The Barnabas in Schools website offers a free download of lesson resources related to the King James Version of the Bible, and the first chapter (pages 12–17) provides specific teaching material on Psalm 23 that enables pupils to explore its meaning and then plan a dramatic performance of the poem. See www.barnabasinschools.org.uk/openingupthekingjamesbible/.

Literacy: Drama and dialect

Age 5–7 and 8–11: 'He ain't heavy...'

The story of the four friends who bring another friend to Jesus on a stretcher is one of the most famous miracle stories in the Bible and lends itself to development in drama.

See a lesson plan for exploring this story with 5–7s and 8–11s on the Barnabas in Schools website: www.barnabasinschools.org.uk/dependence-supporting-each-other/.

Age 8–11: 'Stretcher bearers' as a dramatic poem

Show a photograph of stretcher bearers from the First World War, sourced from Google Images. Together, discuss what you can see in the picture. What interesting questions can we ask about it? Then share out copies of the poem 'To stretcher bearers' by Geoffrey Studdert Kennedy, available at www.poemhunter.com/poem/to-stretcher-bearers.

Explain that Geoffrey wrote this poem from his experiences of working as a chaplain on the front line. It recreates the dialect speech of two stretcher bearers as they gently transport a casualty back to base hospital, and adds a profound comment at the end that references Jesus' challenging words in Matthew 25:40.

Read a section of the poem aloud together, trying to get the dialect right. Are there any unfamiliar words or pronunciations? What do they mean? (A 'Blighty' is a wound bad enough to get you evacuated to a safe rest-camp in Britain but not bad enough to kill you.) Bear in mind that this is a conversation between two men as they carry someone. Who says what? Are they simply saying alternate lines? Imagine one of the soldiers is younger and one older. (The person on the stretcher doesn't speak.) Then set the children the task of planning a paired 'live reading', allocating lines, choosing certain words to emphasise and adding changes in volume and facial expression as appropriate (adding underlines or symbols to the written text). At the end, ask volunteers to share their performances.

History: The Battle of the Somme, 1 July 1916

Richard H. Tawney was a Christian who later became an economist and a Labour politician. As a socialist, he refused to join the British Army as an officer, joining instead as a private but rapidly being promoted to Sergeant in the 20th Manchester Regiment, which took part in the Battle of the Somme. On the first day, Tawney was seriously wounded but was then evacuated and repatriated to England. He was fortunate. Of the 120,000 British soldiers who took part in 'The Somme', 20,000 were killed. Of the 820 men in his own unit, only 54 survived the battle unscathed.

What went wrong? The British had hoped that several days of artillery bombardment would break up the entrenched German barbed wire defences, but they didn't. As the British soldiers left their trenches to advance in their thousands, the German machine-gunners (well protected in their shelters) emerged ready to meet them. The Germans built their positions well and defended them bravely, losing even more soldiers than the British, but the result was, yet again, a cruel stalemate, which ended only as new tactics and weapons (especially tanks) were introduced. Despite the British Army's meticulous planning for the battle, their medical services were overwhelmed with casualties.

Richard Tawney recalled what it was like to go 'over the top' at 7.30 am on the first day of the Battle of the Somme. He and his men had to advance nearly two miles across No Man's Land to attack German positions. At first, things seemed to go well, but then the machine guns started firing. Richard saw many British soldiers killed or wounded. This is his own description, written a month afterwards, of how it feels to be shot (from 'The Attack').

* * *

I don't know what most men feel like when they're wounded. What I felt was I had been hit by a tremendous iron hammer, swung by a giant of inconceivable strength, and then twisted with a sickening sort of wrench so that my head and back banged on the ground, and my feet struggled as though they didn't belong to me. For a second or two my breath wouldn't come. I thought—if that's the right word—'This is death,' and hoped it wouldn't take long. By-and-by, as nothing happened, it seemed I couldn't be dying. When I felt the ground beside me, my fingers closed on the nose-cap of a shell. It was still hot, and I thought absurdly, in a muddled way, 'This is what has got me.'

I tried to turn on my side, but the pain, when I moved, was like a knife, and stopped me dead. There was nothing to do but lie on my back. After a minute two men in my platoon crawled back past me at a few yards distance. They saw me, and seemed to be laughing, though of course they weren't, but they didn't stop. Probably they were wounded. I could have cried at their being so cruel. It's being cut off from human beings that's as bad as anything when one's copped it badly, and, when a lad wriggled up to me and asked, 'What's up, Sergeant?' I loved him. I said, 'Not dying, I think, but pretty bad,' and he wriggled on. What else could he do?

I raised my knees to ease the pain in my stomach, and at once bullets came over; so I put them down. Not that I much minded dying now or thought about it. By a merciful arrangement, when one's half-dead the extra plunge doesn't seem very terrible…

How I longed for the evening! I'd lost my watch, so I tried to tell the time by the sun, cautiously shifting my tin hat off my eyes to have a peep. It stood straight overhead in an enormous arch of blue. After an age I looked again. It still stood in the same place… I began to shout feebly for stretcher bearers, calling out the name of my battalion and division, as though that would bring men running from all points of the compass. Of course it was imbecilic and cowardly. They couldn't hear me, and if they could, they oughtn't to have come… But I'd lost my self-respect. I hoped I should faint, but I couldn't.

It was a lovely evening, and a man stood beside me. I caught him by the ankle, in terror lest he should vanish. In answer to his shouts—he was an R.A.M.C. Corporal—a doctor came and looked at me… I did so want to be spoken kindly to, and I began to whimper, partly to myself, partly aloud… He can't have been more than 26 or 27; but his face seemed to shine with love and comprehension… He listened like an angel while I told him a confused nonsensical yarn about being hit in the back by a nose-cap. Then he said I had been shot with a rifle-bullet through the chest and abdomen, put a stiff bandage round me, and gave me morphia. Anyway, there was nothing more he could do. No stretcher bearers were to hand, so it was out of the question to get me in that night. But after I had felt that divine compassion flow over me, I didn't care. I was like a dog kicked and bullied by everyone that's at last found a kind master, and in a grovelling kind of way I worshipped him.

* * *

Age 7–11: Thinking about feelings

Show pupils appropriate images of soldiers engaging in the Battle of the Somme, then share this passage with them, adding that Richard was eventually taken to hospital and survived the war. Afterwards, set pupils the task of listing together any things that surprise or puzzle them about what he wrote. If they could ask him three interesting questions today about this incident, what would they be? What might his answers be?

What can we learn from this passage about what it was like to be in the battle on that day?

List some words that describe the different feelings Richard had after being shot. What does this tell you about the shock people can go into when they suffer a serious injury? What does someone in shock need?

Discuss: Richard seems to be criticising himself as he describes his experience. Why do you think he does that? Also, why do you think he wanted to write about it afterwards?

Twice, Richard uses the words 'love' and 'loved'. Do you find that embarrassing? Why? (For further discussion, read Paul's definition of love in 1 Corinthians 13. Which of these lines do you think refers to the kind of love that Richard, as a Christian, is describing?)

Citizenship: How to save a life

Age 7–11: Emergency first aid

A variety of charities continue to go into war zones to provide emergency care for those in need. The Red Cross (ICRC) supplies a range of teaching resources for older pupils on this theme, providing practical advice about what to do in emergency situations: see www.redcross.org.uk/What-we-do/Teaching-resources.

St John Ambulance also offer training for young people in first aid: see www.sja.org.uk/sja/young-people.aspx.

Personal and Social Education/Circle Time: Love

Age 7–11: The meaning of love

'Love' can mean many things. Richard's memoir shows what compassion can do when someone is feeling vulnerable, so this session aims to broaden your pupils' understanding of the word. Begin by asking them, in pairs, to discuss three things they 'love'. Feed back answers, listing some on the board. Draw attention to the wide variety of things we 'love', including chocolate!

Explain that 'love' is a word that can mean very different things. (When we say we 'love' chocolate, we're only really saying we like it very much.) Some languages have different words for different kinds of love. The ancient Greeks had a love-word for strong friendships, another for love within a family, and so on. They had one special word for the kind of love that you could share with any other person: *agape* (pronounced a-ga-pay). Agape-love is the kind of powerful, generous love that we see when someone does something really kind for someone else. Agape-love isn't a feeling: it's something good you do for someone else, without wanting anything in return.

In pairs, study the list of things we 'love' on the board. Discuss which of them could be described as agape-love. Then tell your partner about someone you know who has done something very kind for you, or something kind you did for someone else. Feed back, asking pupils how that act of love made them feel afterwards. Draw out in the closing discussion that love is more than a feeling: it's something people do, and it can be very powerful. It makes others feel very special. (Have you done something loving in the last few days?)

THOUGHT FOR THE DAY

The apostle Paul wrote, 'I would be nothing, unless I loved others' (1 Corinthians 13:2). Ask pupils to flex their fingers, then show their hands. Say, 'We can use our hands to hurt other people or to help them. How could you use your hands to help someone else today?' Then ask your pupils to shut their eyes. Repeat Paul's words, then ask the children to think of someone they could help with their hands and show love to today.

Prayer

Father God, help us all to love each other more, showing compassion for all who need it. Amen

Waiting for a train

*

— UNIT 8 —

Waiting for a train: 'Woodbine Willie' and other military chaplains

Background for teachers

Military chaplains are clergy attached to the armed forces. They have a range of responsibilities, but when the First World War began, Church of England chaplains were unclear about their role. Some thought it was about maintaining troop morale in the 'rest' areas, since going to the front line was forbidden to them (although some disobeyed). Roman Catholic chaplains were different. Many dedicated themselves to saving souls, actively preparing those in their charge to meet their Maker. They had to stay with their soldiers (even sharing a dug-out in the trenches), because their job included giving the Last Rites to those facing death. This made a crucial difference because the soldiers respected anyone who shared the same dangers as the people they served.

'Woodbine Willie' (Geoffrey Studdert Kennedy) was a famous Church of England chaplain whose idiosyncratic charisma provided inspiration for many. Initially enthusiastic about the war, he became increasingly cynical but spent as much time as possible with the soldiers, giving out Bibles and cigarettes to anyone who would take them, doing all he could to comfort them in their terror and pain. Later, he became a stretcher bearer (as many other chaplains did), going out into No Man's Land to search for the wounded, give first aid, stay with them under fire to give comfort as they died, or bury the dead.

When a new chaplain asked Geoffrey for advice, he said this:

Live with the men; go everywhere they go. Make up your mind you will share all their risks, and more if you can do any good. The line is the key to the whole business. Work in the very front, and they will listen to you; but if you stay behind, you're wasting your time. Men will forgive you anything but lack of courage and devotion.

STORY RETELLING: WAITING FOR A TRAIN

Albert yawned. He and his mates were hanging around a railway station somewhere in the middle of France, with nothing to do. They'd arrived early in the morning, having marched through the night when it was still dark and cold, wondering what would happen next. But nothing had happened next. There was no train waiting, so they'd been dismissed, told to keep near the station but stay out of trouble, and left to fend for themselves as the morning grew light. It wouldn't be long before the train came; then they'd all be packed on it and taken to the front line and the war.

Would they be coming back? Everyone in the village back home had cheered when Albert and his mates had joined up, signing the papers and promising to serve the King. There had been a parade as they marched away down the high street, with speeches and a brass band from the colliery. What had they played? 'Rule Britannia', or something like that.

There had been a long train journey, uniforms, three hard months of 'boot camp' to turn them into proper soldiers, then another train, and a ship taking them across the English Channel. Albert had never been on a boat that size before. Then there'd been another camp in France, with real training, and machine guns firing real bullets, with trenches and barbed wire to crawl under. Now they were going to see the real thing. What would it be like? As he wandered away from the station and past the strange-looking French houses, he realised he was shivering.

Some of his mates had found an *estiamet* (a kind of pub for soldiers) that had opened in the early morning to catch the passing trade, and were sitting inside drinking red wine and laughing. Albert hadn't joined them. He didn't touch alcohol. Nobody did, in his church back home. He wondered what they were doing now. It was Sunday, after all, not that it seemed to make any difference here. He drifted along the little street and saw a coffee shop that seemed to be open too. At last— somewhere warm! As he went in, he heard a loud crash. Someone was thumping out a tune on the keys of a piano, singing away in a loud Irish voice, surrounded by a crowd of soldiers. Whoever it was couldn't play well, but it didn't matter. It was something to sing along to. Albert bought a coffee at the counter and joined them.

It was an officer! But officers didn't play the piano for their men—they had their own places. Then he looked at the piano player's collar: he was a chaplain! They were singing 'It's a long way to Tipperary' very loudly. After that, the piano player sat back and said with a croaky voice, 'That's me done, lads! You've sung me out!' Loud cheers all round. But then he got up where everyone could see him, touched his clerical collar and said, 'Listen, lads, I'm here to help in any way I can. Sometimes it comforts wives and mothers to hear from me that I have seen their loved ones and talked to them, so here's what I can do.'

He held up a sheaf of little printed letters. 'This says I've seen you, and you're looking well.' He stopped and stared with bulging eyes, shaking his head. 'And now I've heard you too. Good GRIEF!' Everyone laughed. He held up a pile of envelopes. 'You write their addresses on these, and I'll send the letters to anyone you want. You know they read newspaper reports, but it's not enough. They want to know you're all right, don't they?' Lots of men nodded earnestly. 'All right, then. You write down those addresses, we'll collect them in, and we'll pray for our families together, and maybe sing a hymn if you're up for it. Is that all right?' It was, and he handed them out.

The men were soon crowding round with newly addressed envelopes, some showing photographs of their loved ones—a mother here, a family portrait there, or a daughter, a bright girl's face above a clean white blouse. With all the envelopes collected in a basket, the chaplain held them up for all to see and said, 'Let's pray.' Caps doffed, heads bowed, they prayed to God to look after their families, whispering the names of their parents, their wives, their brothers and sisters, and their children. When they'd said, 'Amen,' the chaplain went back to the piano and they all sang, 'The Lord's my shepherd, I'll not want. He makes me down to lie in pastures green; he leadeth me the quiet waters by…' At the end, there was a long silence in the coffee house, as if for a moment a door had been opened into another place, cleaner and better.

Then whistles were blowing in the street outside. Regimental sergeants strode past, shouting their orders, telling the men to muster, getting ready to board the troop train in 30 minutes. There was a sudden scurrying of soldiers looking for rifles, helmets and packs.

'Padre,' said Albert, as he shouldered his pack, 'how often do you do this? Every Sunday?'

The chaplain sighed. 'Every day, lad, week after week.' He

gently placed the basket of envelopes on a table behind the piano.

'Why?'

'Because, for now, it's the best I can do.' He picked up two large, heavy knapsacks full of Bibles and cigarettes. 'Come on, then. Can't keep the train waiting, can we?'

Religious Education: 'Woodbine Willie'

Geoffrey Studdert Kennedy got his nickname from the Woodbine cigarettes that he gave out to soldiers with his Bibles. At the time, cigarettes weren't thought to be bad for your health. In fact, many soldiers took up smoking because it kept them warm during a cold night in the trenches, and cigarettes smelt better than many other things left lying around on the battlefield.

Age 5–7: Writing a prayer

Tell Albert's story, making changes as appropriate for the age group. What sort of prayers do we think Woodbine Willie prayed with the men in that café once he had collected in all the letters? Ask pupils to compose their own prayer that might be prayed by a soldier, thinking of his family and friends at home. What would he wish for them?

Give younger pupils envelopes on which to draw the face of someone they are thinking about who might be sad. The envelopes could be hung or pegged on a 'prayer tree' in a quiet corner, equipped with paper, envelopes and pens as a place where children can go to think quiet thoughts. The book *Creative Ideas for Quiet Corners* by Lynn Chambers (Barnabas, 2008) has many more suggestions for developing this idea and can be purchased as a download (see www.barnabasinchurches.org.uk/9781841016559Z/).

Age 8–11: Where is God in all this?

Set the children the task of discussing the question 'What or who is God?', asking them to list answers on sticky notes. Collate the notes on a display board, grouping similar responses and adding further prompts to create a wider range as necessary.

Explain that during the First World War, many people found that their ideas about God were changing. They were asking, was God someone who looked after you, protecting all the good people? That kind of God didn't seem to be there on the battlefield or in the hospital. After these experiences, many people had no use for a God who didn't seem to be protecting them, and they gave up on 'religion'. Perhaps he was a cruel monster. (Was their idea of God too small?) But others found their faith being enriched. It made sense of things and gave hope where nothing else could.

Like many others, Geoffrey supported the war initially, believing that God wanted the Germans defeated, but his opinion changed in the trenches, when he saw what war was really like. Did God *really* want all these awful deaths? Geoffrey's Christian beliefs changed: now, he could only make sense of God by imagining him suffering along with the human race and all creation. God didn't want people to be fighting like this, but he couldn't stop them, either. The only way God could make a difference was by coming to earth as Jesus, suffering on the cross and providing a way for people to be changed, one by one, into new people who knew God personally. If they accepted his help, people could start again. As Jesus came back to life, so could they. It was the only way God could change the world—one person at a time.

Set pupils the task of drawing a simple cross, offering a choice of titles such as 'The big question', 'The suffering God' or 'For God so loved the world'. Ask them to write, 'I chose this title because...' and then copy this sentence: 'Christians believe that Jesus died on the cross to save people from the things that spoil their lives.'

Offer sentence starters to get the pupils developing their own thoughts on this key Christian idea.

- 'If God could die on a cross, it might mean...'
- 'If Jesus was God in human form, then...'
- 'I think the cross is a key Christian symbol because...'
- 'My biggest question about the cross is...'

Literacy: Woodbine Willie's own thoughts

The story is based on Geoffrey's own words about how he tried to help the soldiers waiting to be sent to the front. As the soldiers were getting on the train, he joined them, giving out cigarettes and Bibles. This is how he described it in a letter:

I begin at the top of the train; and work down it, going into each carriage. I look round into their faces. I can always tell the man who has taken that trip before. You can see it in his eyes... so for an hour (it always stands an hour) with the knapsacks (of Bibles and cigarettes) growing lighter and a lump in the throat that grows bigger. Often I have to cling on to finish the last carriages, creeping along the footboard. At last, I am left alone (on the station platform) looking after the disappearing tail-lights. There is nothing glorious about the departure. It is all disgusting and filthy. God only knows the hardships men endure on these journeys in packed and dirty carriages. No place to wash, no place to move, they sit and wait for eighteen hours or more until, I suppose, they hear far off the sound of guns and know that the end is near.

Geoffrey wrote many poems to explain his thoughts about the war and where God was to be found in it all. Some can be found at www.poemhunter.com/geoffrey-anketell-studdert-kennedy/poems.

Age 5–7: Responding to 'Worry'

Share the poem 'Worry' with the class (see www.poemhunter.com/poem/worry-23).

It's about a soldier who has been blinded in a battle, wondering about his future when the war is over. Together, discuss the poem's rhyme scheme and its use of odd spellings and phrases to capture the colloquial speech of the soldier. Explain that Geoffrey met many wounded soldiers like this man; the poem was probably based on a real conversation. After sharing it, pick out key words and phrases that describe what the soldier is worried about. Does this poem have a message for people back home? (The Earl Haig Fund's Poppy Appeal was set up to care for wounded ex-servicemen.) Do we know what jobs can be done by blind people today (for example, government minister)?

Set the task of writing your own poem about buying a poppy and what it means, or about worry itself, perhaps as an acrostic.

Age 8–11: Responding to 'Waste' and other poems

After the war, Geoffrey wrote this poem, entitled 'Waste':

Waste of Muscle, waste of Brain,
Waste of Patience, waste of Pain,
Waste of Manhood, waste of Health,
Waste of Beauty, waste of Wealth,
Waste of Blood, and waste of Tears,
Waste of Youth's most precious years,
Waste of ways the Saints have trod,
Waste of Glory, waste of God—War!

Together, discuss the structure of the poem, its use of repetition, the rhyme scheme, the metre (which perhaps mimics the sound of soldiers marching) and the use of capital letters to highlight significant words. Then contrast this by studying, and maybe singing, the lyrics of a popular hymn of the time: 'Onward, Christian soldiers'. Can your pupils spot Geoffrey's sly reference to the hymn in his penultimate line? What do they think he would say if he were invited to speak at a Remembrance Day service, and someone wanted to include that hymn? What do they think the last line of his poem means? (Point out that most Christians today wouldn't sing this hymn; 'Make me a channel of your peace' is far more popular.)

Write a letter from Geoffrey Kennedy to the person planning the service who wants to sing that hymn, explaining what you think would be Geoffrey's own thoughts.

Extension

Pupils could study other poems by Geoffrey Kennedy, such as:

- 'Solomon in all his glory' (www.poemhunter.com/poem/solomon-in-all-his-glory)
- 'What's the use of a cross to 'im?' (www.poemhunter.com/poem/what-s-the-use-of-a-cross-to-im)

History: Military chaplains

Chaplains came from a variety of denominations and found different ways of serving the men in their care. Many soldiers took great comfort from their ministry.

Age 5–7: Toc H

Discuss: if you've been very busy or upset, what do you do to calm yourself down? Sometimes, people need more than sleep, especially if they've been very tired and scared for a long time. The soldiers of the First World War could be fighting in the trenches for weeks, being shelled or shot at. If you'd been given the day off a few miles away from the battlefield, what sorts of things would you want to do to help you 'switch off'? What sort of place would help you calm down? (Together, list a few possibilities on the board.) Many soldiers tried to forget their troubles by getting drunk, which didn't really help, but one chaplain tried to give them something different.

Philip 'Tubby' Clayton was a Church of England chaplain (East Kent and Bedfordshires) based in the Belgian town of Poperinge, which was a crossroads for many soldiers who were either on their way out to the battlefield or coming back. Another chaplain gave him the idea of creating some kind of rest home for off-duty soldiers, which didn't serve alcohol but offered something better. Clayton found a large damaged house for rent, had it repaired and opened it in December 1915. Talbot House (or Toc H) was open to men and officers alike. Once inside, no one was addressed by their rank but only by their first and last names, which was very unusual. (Other establishments were reserved either for officers or other ranks.) It had a library, a large tea room and a beautiful walled garden where men could sit and forget about the war for a while. The attic was converted into a chapel known as the 'Upper Room' for church services.

Clayton tried to produce a 'home-from-home' effect by using colourful rugs and as many vases of flowers as possible. He also organised debates, concerts and a message service so that soldiers could keep in touch with each other.

Set pupils the task of creating a poster advertising Toc H to soldiers passing through Poperinge. What words and phrases would encourage them to come along and rest? How could they explain that everybody would be treated the same once they came inside? What images or motifs would help to explain what the place was there for?

Toc H still exists as a Christian charity (see www.toch-uk.org.uk/index.html).

Age 8–11: Father Willie Doyle (8th Royal Dublin Fusiliers)

The outbreak of the First World War temporarily defused an impending Irish civil war between the (mainly Roman Catholic) Nationalists and (mainly Protestant) Unionists. Ireland provided 206,000 volunteers for the British Army, both Catholic and Protestant. The two Christian denominations tended to keep to their own battalions and have their own chaplains, but one Catholic chaplain's ministry had a powerful impact across the denominational divide. Willie Doyle was a complex character whose spirituality rivalled that of those early Christian saints who delighted in physical hardship as a road to holiness—but it prepared him well. These extracts are taken from his many letters home.

When accompanying the 8th Royal Dublin Fusiliers as they advanced during the Battle of the Somme in July 1916, he wrote:

A halt for a few minutes gave me the opportunity I was waiting for. I hurried along from group to group, and as I did, men fell on their knees to receive absolution. A few words to give them courage, for no man knew if he would return alive. A 'God bless and protect you, boys,' and I passed on to the next company. As I did, a soldier stepped out of the ranks, caught me by the hand, and said: 'I am not a Catholic, sir, but I want to thank you for that beautiful prayer.' The regiments moved on to the wood, while the doctor and I took up our position in the dressing room to wait for the wounded. This was a dugout on the hill facing Leuze Wood, and had been in German occupation the previous afternoon...

Fighting was going on all around, so that I was kept busy, but all the time my thoughts and my heart were with my poor boys in the wood opposite. They had reached it safely, but the Germans had somehow worked round the sides and temporarily cut them off... Under the circumstances it would be madness to try and reach the wood, but my heart bled for the wounded and dying lying there alone. When dusk came I made up my mind to try and creep through the valley, more especially as the fire had slackened very much. As I was setting out I met a sergeant who argued the point with me. 'You can do little good, Father,' he said, 'down there in the wood, and will only run a great risk. Wait till night comes and then we shall be able to bring all the wounded up here. Don't forget that, although we have plenty of officers, we have only one priest to look after us.' The poor fellow was so much in earnest I decided to wait a little while at least.

In June 1917, during the Battle of Messines, he wrote:

Once again I had evidence of the immense confidence our men have in their priest. It was quite evident that they were rapidly becoming demoralised, as the best of troops will who have to remain inactive under heavy shellfire. Little groups were running from place to place for greater shelter, and the officers seemed to have lost control. I walked along the line of men, crouching behind the sandbag wall, and was amused to see the ripple of smiles light up the terrified lads' faces (so many were mere boys) as I went by. By the time I got back again the men were laughing and chatting as if all danger was miles away, for quite unintentionally, I had given them courage by walking along without my gas mask or steel helmet, both of which I had forgotten in my hurry.

Father Doyle was killed by a shell during the third battle of Ypres, on 16 August 1917. A Belfast Orangeman wrote in a letter to the *Glasgow Weekly News*, 1 September 1917:

Father Doyle was a good deal among us. We couldn't possibly agree with his religious opinions, but we simply worshipped him for other things. He didn't know the meaning of fear, and he didn't know what bigotry was. He was as ready to risk his life to take a drop of water to a wounded Ulsterman as to assist men of his own faith and regiment. If he risked his life looking after Ulster Protestant soldiers once, he did it a hundred times in his last few days. The Ulstermen felt his loss more keenly than anybody, and none were readier to show their marks of respect to the dead hero priest than were our Ulster Presbyterians. Father Doyle was a true Christian in every sense of the word, and a credit to any religious faith.

Using these extracts, list the different things that Willie Doyle did on the battlefield. Which do you think the soldiers valued most, and why? What does this tell you about soldiers' lives on the Western Front? Why do you think the religious divides didn't seem to matter so much to Irish soldiers once they were on the battlefield?

Personal and Social Education/Circle Time: Encouragement

Age 5–11: Learning something new

Part of a chaplain's job is simply to 'be' with people who are struggling. Encouragement is about 'giving courage' to someone who needs it. Begin this session by trying to demonstrate a new skill (such as juggling) in class… badly. Note pupil reactions. As you fail, respond by apparently getting cross with yourself.

Explain that life isn't always easy. We all need a bit of encouragement when we start something new. It can look a bit funny if somebody tries to do something, then fails—but think about what your laughter does to that person inside. If somebody was learning how to ride a bike and people laughed every time they fell over, then what could happen? (They might give up.) Why do some people like to tease others like this? (To make themselves feel bigger or better.)

Think of a time when you were nervous about trying to do something new and it was difficult as well, but in the end you succeeded. Was there someone who helped you to keep going, so that you didn't give up? It may have been a parent, another child or someone else. What did they do? What did they say? (Discuss with partners, then feed back.) All those people helped you to be brave. They gave you encouragement. Did you know that 'courage' is a word that comes from French? It means 'having a big heart'. So those people gave you a bit of strength in your heart to keep going.

Set the task of drawing a large heart in the middle of a page, with a face drawn on it, looking nervous. Next to the heart, draw something that's difficult to do. Round the heart, draw speech bubbles containing comments that encourage somebody to try again and not 'lose heart'. Afterwards, share the encouraging comments that we can make.

THOUGHT FOR THE DAY

We are all here to encourage each other. Encouraging people makes the world a better place for everyone. Who could you encourage today?

Prayer

Father God, give me courage when the world is rough. Help me to be strong for others too. Amen

'Her face is the fairest'

*

'Her face is the fairest': Nurses and VADs caring for the sick and wounded

Background for teachers

Compared with other countries in 1914, British Army plans for medical care were advanced. A soldier wounded on the Western Front could be back in 'Blighty' within 48 hours, receiving state-of-the-art care. (This is impressive even by today's standards.) However, these plans didn't take into account the way modern warfare was developing, especially when it came to handling large numbers of casualties arriving all at once—as they did in the Battle of the Somme. Field hospitals were often placed too far back from the front lines, so, after receiving first aid, casualties could face a long, difficult journey by stretcher before seeing a doctor. Given the primitive state of antibiotics, the manure-rich farmland in which the battles were being fought, and the often atrocious conditions of trench warfare, it is not surprising that general sickness and infection became a bigger killer than all the bullets, shells, bombs and gas put together.

However, nursing care had also come a long way since the days of Florence Nightingale. Professional nurses were supported by many unpaid but highly trained helpers known as VADs (Volunteer Auxiliary Duties). They performed an amazing service, both close to the battlefield and further back in hospitals and convalescence homes. VADs weren't meant to replace nurses but they became invaluable as hospitals became overloaded with thousands of the war-wounded and sick.

STORY RETELLING: 'HER FACE IS THE FAIREST'

Katie really didn't like the Scottish sergeant. He'd been brought into the hospital with several bullet wounds in the arms and legs that were healing well, but there was something about him that slightly scared her. Whenever she walked by, his dark eyes seemed to stare right through her and see someone else. Of course, as a volunteer auxiliary, she was there to 'like' all the soldiers who came in. Being wounded is shocking and horrible, and all these young men needed to know that somebody cared and wanted them to get better, but this sergeant had a hardness about him that made her wish he would get better soon and be gone. He looked like someone who found it easy to get into trouble.

With the other soldiers, though, he was fine. When they had a singalong, his rich baritone voice carried them all along, especially when they sang old Scottish songs like 'Loch Lomond'. 'Oh, ye'll take the high road and I'll take the low road…' He could raise the roof when he was in the mood, but all the time there seemed to be something angry inside him that he was holding back, keeping in check. Katie once asked him to sing 'Annie Laurie', a favourite of hers, but his eyes seemed to flash in fury. 'Don't go there,' they said silently. 'That song's none of your business.' She didn't ask again. The other nurses and auxiliaries agreed he was an odd sort but told her not to worry about it.

'He's probably seen some terrible things,' said Sister McIndoe, who was in charge of the ward. 'Don't take it personally.' They were wise words, and there were many other patients to care about, some coming in with terrible wounds. There were things Katie had never thought she'd see, not in all her training, but she was here to help, and that was it. Her days were spent removing filthy uniforms from patients (sometimes very carefully with sharp scissors), cleaning dirty bedclothes, washing wounds, replacing dressings—and, whenever she could, sharing a kind word with anyone who needed it. There was more to healing a person than just cleaning their wounds and leaving them lying there. 'Always try to have a smile for everybody, even when you don't feel like it,' said Sister McIndoe. 'Remember, girls, those young men are looking to see how you react to them. Don't look away, even if you're shocked. They need to know they're still people, even when their bodies are broken.'

This evening had been different. First of all, there'd been that business with the newspaper—some nasty story about German soldiers shooting British prisoners, which was against all the rules of war. 'That's evil!' exclaimed Katie as a soldier read it out. 'You can't shoot prisoners!' The others all agreed loudly, but she noticed the sergeant suddenly going quiet, turning away and staring up at the ceiling—and, just like that, she realised. 'You've done that too,' she thought. 'You've shot some Germans you'd taken prisoner.' She didn't know what to think. In this war, British soldiers were meant to be the good ones, weren't they?

Then a new patient was brought in with some horrible head wounds. She hated dealing with those, trying to clean up someone's face, especially when the man was in awful pain when you touched him, but it was all part of the job. The soldiers in the ward knew how she felt and admired the way she stuck at it, but then, as Katie started peeling off the man's bandages and dabbing his face with water, she heard something new. At the other end of the ward, the sergeant was singing.

Her brow is like the snowdrift, her neck is like the swan
Her face is the fairest that e'er the sun shone on
That e'er the sun shone on and dark blue is her eye
And for bonnie Annie Laurie I'd lay me down and die...

It was 'Annie Laurie'. The sergeant knew she hated doing this task and, in his own way, as she started trying to sort out the wounds on a man's broken face, the sergeant was trying to help.

* * *

After sharing the story, ask the pupils to discuss and share any interesting questions that might be asked about the story, which is based on a true incident.

Religious Education: Healing the troubled

Age 5–7: Touching the broken

Discuss why we don't like it if we see someone feeling ill or caught in an accident. Explain that nurses and other carers might not like it either but they make it their job to sort out what's wrong, because someone has to.

Then, using an age-appropriate version, share the Bible story of what happened when Jesus encountered someone with a dreaded skin disease (Mark 1:40–45). Begin by wondering what it might be like to have something wrong with your body that scares everybody else away. (Others might be scared of catching the disease—or might just seeing its effects be upsetting?) Then try acting out a traditional reaction to diseases like leprosy—to make the 'sufferer' ring a bell, and avoid them if they come down the street. Sit all the children down, then either walk around ringing a bell to incur the reaction or give this task to a child. In pairs, discuss what it would feel like to be treated like that. Then tell the Bible story, drawing attention to the way Jesus 'felt compassion' for the man. (The original Greek verb means a feeling like anger.) Then he reached out and touched the man. Of course, from the story we know that the man was healed, but focus instead on how he must have felt to be touched by someone who cared. (Note: did the man ask to be touched? No.) What might this story have to say about the way we treat someone who is unwell?

Afterwards, set the task of creating a 'get well' card that could be sent to someone who is ill. (What is the most important thing this card is meant to say? Could you convey that message without words, if you had to? How?) Younger children might appreciate the use of a 'home corner' set up as a hospital, where they can role-play being doctors, paramedics and nurses.

Age 8–11: Healing music

In the story 'Her face is the fairest', a song touches someone deeply. Music can have a powerful effect on human emotions, and there's a fascinating Bible story about how the young David was introduced to a rather disturbed King Saul to offer him music therapy (1 Samuel 16:14–23).

Mozart's Clarinet Quintet is just one piece that touches people deeply. Play either this or another piece of classical music (without words), setting pupils the challenge of listening to it. First, ask them to 'conduct' a couple of minutes of the music with their fingers and hands as the music plays, possibly with their eyes shut. Then develop this activity with pencil and paper, encouraging pupils to allow their pencils to move across the paper as the music changes, drawing whatever the music makes them think of: they might simply make patterns. (If this music was the soundtrack to a film, you could ask, 'What do you think would be happening on the screen?') Challenge pupils to keep listening as they do this.

You could contrast this music with a restful piece of classical worship music, such as a Gregorian chant. Encourage pupils to talk about what music 'does' for them. Is there a favourite song or other piece of music that cheers them up, calms them down or just leaves them feeling happy? Explain that there's a part of the brain that can still hear music when we are asleep, so it's important to listen to calming music towards bedtime if we want to get any rest.

In one of his letters, Paul says, 'Whatever is true, whatever is noble, whatever is right, whatever is pure, whatever is lovely, whatever is admirable—if anything is excellent or praiseworthy—think about such things' (Philippians 4:8, NIV).

Set pupils the challenge of writing about a piece of music that they think is pure, lovely and excellent, saying why they think it so. (You might want to provide the class with a succession of pieces over a given week, so that they can select a favourite.) Encourage them to discuss the different elements of the piece, such as melody, harmony, beat, bass and lyrics, and to describe especially how it makes them feel.

Literacy: Reading letters from Indian soldiers

The British Army was a strikingly multicultural, multinational force, with large contingents volunteering from India, Canada, Australia, New Zealand and many other nations. As part of the British Empire, India provided over 1.27 million men, all volunteers, of whom 827,000 were combatants. British medical care was generally appreciated by wounded Empire servicemen. Under royal patronage, the exotically designed Brighton Pavilion was converted into a hospital serving the Indian war-wounded, making a strong impression on those being treated there.

Isar Singh (Sikh, 59th rifles) writes to a friend from the Indian General Hospital, Brighton Pavilion:

Do not be anxious about me. We are very well looked after. White soldiers are always beside our beds—day and night. We get very good food four times a day. We also get milk. Our hospital is in the place where the King used to have his throne. Every man is washed once a day in hot water. The King has given a strict order that no trouble be given to any Indian soldier in hospital. Men in hospital are tended like flowers, and the King and Queen sometimes come to visit them.

A wounded Sikh soldier from India writes from hospital in England to his father in the Punjab:

(20 February 1915) Here the ladies tend us wounded, as a mother tends her child. They pour milk into our mouths, when our own parents, brothers and sisters, were we ill, would only give us water in a pot. Here you see the brotherhood of the English, who are kind to us without further motive. The ladies are so kind, they even carry off our excreta; and if we need any food or drink, they put it in our mouths. They wash our bedclothes every week and massage our backs when they ache from lying in bed.

They put us in motor cars and take us through the city. When, at four o'clock, we go out from the hospital, the ladies of the city give us fruit. They say, 'We have never seen such men. We have only heard that they are the Sikhs of India who once fought against England. Now we see them with our own eyes.' They cheer us for beating the Germans in battle. Their kings say, 'Brothers, what matter of men are the Indians?'

Senior Assistant Surgeon J.N. Godbole, writing to a friend in Bombay from No. 8 Indian General Hospital, Bournemouth, says:

(18 March 1915) The people here are of a very amiable disposition. They talk pleasantly, treat us kindly, and are pleased to see us. We do not hear bad language from the white people here, as we do in India. But this only applies to those who have not seen India. Those who have been to India gnash their teeth at us; some laugh and make fun; but there are not many who do this. The people here are charming. It is impossible to say why they become so bad on reaching India.

Age 5–7: Reading letters about medical care

Share the first two letters. Explain that these soldiers had never seen England before. What do their letters tell us about the medical care they received? Try to list at least four things that they appreciated, then rank them in order, placing the most important thing first.

'Flag days' often raised funds for charities such as those helping the war-wounded. The printed paper 'flags' were small enough to be pinned to the lapel of a coat. Design a flag for 'Indian Soldiers Flag Day', using popular Indian motifs of the time, such as a tiger or elephant, or a Sikh soldier in British uniform, wearing the traditional turban.

Age 8–11s: Reading a letter about prejudice

Share all three letters, noting the contrasting tone in the third letter, which mentions the difference in the behaviour to Indian soldiers by some British people who had themselves been to India. Explain that at the time this was written, India was part of the British Empire and some people thought that this meant Indian people weren't as good as British people. However, the Indian volunteers were loyal soldiers whose outstanding contribution to the war was deeply appreciated by many. Discuss these contrasting attitudes. What might this tell us about prejudice? Where could it come from?

Research the names and flags of all the nations that fought in the British Army during the First World War. Use these and appropriate images to create a patriotic poster for the time, celebrating the army's international character, with the title 'Our Empire Stands Together!'

History: Caring for the sick and wounded

The Hague Conventions of 1899 and 1907 were international conferences that tried to establish a set of rules by which wars might be prevented or fairly conducted in future, although not every country was willing to sign up. They included guidance about caring for prisoners of war, including the sick. When these rules were followed, they made a great impact.

Age 5–7: A nurse

One British soldier (Private H. Turner, 50th Division, Machine Gun Corps) was taken prisoner by the Germans and fell sick with dysentery, which makes a person very dehydrated and terribly thirsty. He recalled being treated in prison hospital by Sister Kristina, a nurse who spoke no English but cared very deeply about the wounded men in her care. His account says this:

In our ward there were many nationalities—French, Italian, Russian, Polish, American, as well as British—and all of us were suffering from… dysentery. Each evening, before going off duty, Sister would call at the ward with a big jug of water and ask, 'Wasser trinken?' She was no linguist, but she had taken the trouble to learn the goodnight greetings of the different nationalities in her ward. As she left the room she would say, 'Bonsoir, Franzose; Buona sera, Italiano; Pokoynoy nochee, Russki; Good night, Englander.' And to return the compliment we would chorus back in German, 'Gute Nacht, Schwester.'

Research more ways of saying 'Good night' in different languages, then act out the scene as Sister Kristina walks round saying 'good night' to the soldiers in her care. (The teacher plays Sister Kristina, and the pupils play the soldiers.) Afterwards, ask pupils to discuss why they think she did this for soldiers who were her 'enemy'. Then set the task of writing 'Good night' in different languages next to a picture of Sister Kristina and her jug of water.

Age 8–11: Nurses and VADs

Study the passage used in the previous activity, then share this passage also, from the diary of an Australian nurse serving in the British Army (Sister Elizabeth Nordvan, Australian Army Nursing Service).

Towards the end of the war I had charge of a ward of German prisoners, but they were nearly all kids. We had boys of fourteen crying out for their mothers! The British Army was very severe. They wouldn't allow the boys to write home and tell their mothers that they were sick; they wouldn't allow anything like that. So I got a list of their addresses and I wrote to all their mothers and let them know how they were getting along, and if they were doing well or if they weren't. The letters went through Switzerland and when I came home from the war lots of the mothers wrote to me to say how grateful they were. After all, those mothers were just as worried about their kids as we were about ours… I never hated the Germans. I just loved people—and especially poor sick kids.

Discuss the nurse's reasons for doing this. Imagine you are Sister Elizabeth, serving in British Army Hospital No. 15, somewhere in France. Write a letter to the mother of Bruno Schmidt (aged 14) from Hamburg, who is in her ward with a bullet wound to the leg. The wound is healing nicely but he is feeling really homesick. What do you think his mother needs to hear?

Citizenship: Finding out about charities

Age 7–11: Caring for victims of war

There are many charities set up to care for the victims of war, be they members of the armed forces or civilians. Set pupils the task of researching and presenting the story of how one of these charities was started. Some charities have website resources for children, but do check their nature and content before advocating their use in school. Perhaps you could invite a representative from a local charity to come and talk to the pupils, and make their cause the subject of your next fundraising effort. The following national charities have websites that may be of use, although a local branch or charity may have more relevance to your pupils.

- www.helpforheroes.org.uk/heroes_hat_trick.html. Help for Heroes has a useful PE challenge that gives a hint of what it is like to become suddenly disabled.
- www.britishlegion.org.uk/remembrance/schools-and-learning/ learning-pack. This learning pack is available free from the British Legion and can be used all year.
- www.icrc.org/eng/who-we-are/history/first-world-war/index. jsp. This explains how the Red Cross charity became an international relief organisation during the First World War.

Personal and Social Education/Citizenship/ Circle Time: Caring

Age 5–11: People who care

The best nurses and VADs knew that there was more to helping someone get better than just giving them the right medicine. This session explores how we can show others that we care.

Draw a simple cartoon desert island with a palm tree on the display board. Discuss with the children what it would be like to have to go and live there. (Draw a stick man near the tree.) In pairs, discuss the most important things a person would need. What would you miss having most of all? In feedback, draw out the idea that the one thing we would miss most of all would be having other people who care for us. Explain that people are social: most of the time, we naturally like to be with other people who care for us. In pairs, discuss how you know that someone cares for you, then feed back and list suggestions on the board. (Draw out the idea that caring is something you do, not just feel.)

In their books, pupils should write the word 'Caring' in the middle of the page and, around it, write or draw things they can do to show that they genuinely care for someone. They could place school-related activities on the left-hand side of the page and out-of-school activities on the right. Feed back, and perhaps list for display, some of the pupils' ideas.

THOUGHT FOR THE DAY

In the Bible, Paul wrote about what it means to be really caring, and he called it 'Love'. He said this:

Love never gives up.
Love cares more for others than for self.
Love doesn't want what it doesn't have.
Love doesn't strut,
Doesn't have a swelled head,
Doesn't force itself on others,
Isn't always 'me first',
Doesn't fly off the handle,
Doesn't keep score of the sins of others,
Doesn't revel when others grovel,
Takes pleasure in the flowering of truth,
Puts up with anything,
Trusts God always,
Always looks for the best,
Never looks back,
But keeps going to the end.

1 CORINTHIANS 13:4–7, THE MESSAGE

Prayer

Father God, help me to learn how to care for other people like that.
Amen

The white feather

*

The white feather:
Stephen Hobhouse goes to prison

Background for teachers

Despite the widespread enthusiasm in August 1914 for dashing into uniform, there were pacifists who, for religious and other reasons, thought the whole enterprise immoral, wasteful and cruel. Individual consciences could lead pacifists in very different directions. Some, such as Stephen Hobhouse, refused to have anything to do with the war effort, risking prison and even execution for their beliefs. Others were content to serve in reserved occupations that didn't actively help or hinder the war effort, such as farming. Others, such as William Coltman (see Unit 7), joined the armed forces in non-combatant roles, including being a stretcher bearer on the battlefield. Their decisions came down to their personal beliefs—and having the courage to follow them.

As the war continued, many pacifists found life increasingly difficult and dangerous. Enthusiastic young women would prowl city streets, pinning white feathers on young men who were not in uniform, as a symbol of cowardice. Secret Service employees kept the politically suspect under surveillance, and off-duty soldiers sometimes disrupted pacifist meetings with catcalls and violence. When conscription was introduced in 1916, many 'conscientious objectors' (or 'conchies') were sent to prison for refusing to 'serve their country'.

STORY RETELLING: THE WHITE FEATHER

As prison cells go, Stephen Hobhouse thought, this one wasn't too bad. He'd seen quite a few in three years, some of them incredibly cold or damp, but this one was dry and they'd even given him a mattress to sleep on. Would he be staying here long? A cell like this felt too good for a 'conchie'. In one prison, they'd just given him a plank of wood to sleep on. 'Conchie'. 'Conscientious Objector'. Some people called him a coward because he refused to fight the Germans. Others said he was just being awkward. 'Why don't you do something useful instead, like becoming an ambulance driver or a stretcher bearer?' But Stephen had said 'No' to all of that. 'I'm a Christian,' he'd said. 'I'm not doing anything to support this war. It's all wrong!'

He thought back to the time before they'd locked him up. 'Why aren't you in uniform?' a smart young woman had asked him in the street when he was simply looking in a shop window. 'You should be serving your country!' He'd never seen her before in his life but she seemed very angry with him. 'Because it's wrong,' he sighed. 'Coward!' she snorted, thrusting a white feather into his hand before striding away in disgust.

Then there was the day he'd received the letter telling him he was being conscripted, forced to join the army. 'I'm not going to support this war,' he'd said to the officer at the desk in the recruitment office. 'Don't you want to serve your country?' asked the officer, mystified. Stephen had been put on trial and sent to prison for being a 'deserter'. Strange times. Now, his mother just looked worried when she visited him. For three years, she'd been writing letters to government ministers, trying to get him set free, but nothing happened. His wife Mary visited him faithfully but she'd suffered too. Prison doesn't just affect the people inside the walls. 'Conchies' were often put in 'solitary'—single cells with no one to talk to—for hours. That had given him a lot of time to think about Mary, and it wasn't easy.

There was a rattling of keys at the cell door. 'Prisoner 357!' said the prison warder. 'You have a visitor.' Stephen stood up, glad of a little exercise and the chance to meet another human being, and was led out along the whitewashed corridor. It was odd how every moment outside his cell was now precious, even this. After passing through several doors that needed to be unlocked, they came to the visiting room—and there, accompanied by another guard, was Mary, seated on the other side of a wide table. They'd been married for three years and Stephen had spent most of that time in prison. She was wearing her best coat and dress for him. 'How are you?' she whispered as he sat down.

'The better for seeing you,' he shrugged. 'How's Mother?'

'Fine.' Ten minutes of awkward conversation passed too quickly, then a voice said, 'Time's up!' The warder pointed at a clock on the wall.

'Could I kiss my wife, please?' asked Stephen as he stood up. All of a sudden, he just wanted to touch her and show her he cared.

'It's against regulations, Prisoner 357,' the warder replied. Nodding sadly, they said their goodbyes quickly and Mary turned to leave. He knew she didn't want him to see her crying, and that hurt even more.

After taking the long, sad walk back to his cell, Stephen sat down, his head in his hands, expecting to hear the door slam shut as usual—but it didn't. Now what? He looked up to see the warder standing inside the door, his own eyes filled with tears. 'Begging your pardon, sir, but I had to say that. It's not right. Whatever you've done, forbidding a man to kiss his wife goodbye is just plain wrong. But that's the rules and I have to keep them. I'm sorry.' The man was really upset.

Stephen held out his hand. 'Sir, I've got to say thank you.'

'What for?' asked the warder as he shook Stephen's hand.

'Because you've just restored my faith in people. I was starting to lose it.'

Religious Education: Speaking truth to power

Age 5–7: Suffering for speaking out

Stephen suffered greatly for speaking out. In the Bible, there are many stories exploring the dilemmas of speaking out when everybody else is saying or doing the wrong thing, notably in the tales of Shadrach, Meshach and Abednego (Daniel 3) and Daniel in the lions' den (Daniel 6), where God intervened to justify his people. These are ideal for dramatic storytelling. Read them yourself first, understand the flow of the narrative, and think your way through any 'journeys': will your groups of children 'travel' in the story as the characters do? Where will the key locations be, if you are acting the story out in a larger space? Will you need sound effects or other props?

Begin by acting out some of the feelings in the story, either making faces or statues to illustrate them. Then 'walk through' the story, with small groups of the class saying aloud and repeating the words you give them and copying the gestures and actions that you demonstrate. In both stories, the young men were captured from their homeland and taken into exile by enemy soldiers, imprisoned but then raised in the royal palace as honoured students before being given positions of responsibility. Enemies can whisper and plot against them, guards can (gently) arrest them, and they can speak or act out their defiance. Note the attitude of the kings in both cases, and the way they respond to a servant who doesn't do as he is told. How will you dramatise the fiery furnace or the lions' den? Contrast the kings' responses at the end of each story. Finally, ask your class to discuss what they think is the message of each story. What further questions do they have about the stories?

For older pupils, there is the strange story of the prophet Jeremiah. Speaking the truth can get you into trouble if the people in charge don't want to hear your message, but Jeremiah was determined to be God's messenger, whether people wanted to hear him or not. Like Stephen, he refused to support his country as it prepared for war, and both of them expected the war to go horribly wrong. Using an appropriate children's version, retell the story of what happened to Jeremiah as his nation prepared (with Egyptian support) to fight the invading Babylonian army. As Jeremiah tried to leave the city of Jerusalem, he was captured by his enemies, who tried to silence him by locking him up in prison and then dumped him in a dry well (Jeremiah 37:11–21; 38:1–18, 24–28). Point out how an African adviser (Ebedmelech of Ethiopia) rescued Jeremiah, but King Zedekiah was too scared to challenge the people who wanted the war—and later suffered for it.

Set pupils the task of dividing a page into four rectangles with two lines. Suggest that, in the bottom two sections, they draw Stephen in his cell and Jeremiah stuck at the bottom of the well. In the two sections above, they could draw the two people who helped them—the warder and Ebedmelech. Ask them to show what each person might be thinking, using thought bubbles.

Extension

Both Stephen and Jeremiah believed in God. What do you think God may have been thinking about them?

Age 8–11: Swords into ploughshares?

Explain that at the end of the First World War, many pacifists like Stephen Hobhouse remembered a famous Bible passage and hoped that all the newly invented weapons wouldn't be used again. (Show a picture of an ancient traditional plough, from Google Images.) In the Old Testament, the prophet Isaiah used a simple word-picture to describe a future time of peace when weapons could be turned into something useful because they weren't needed. Swords could be melted down and beaten to make 'ploughshares'—the metal part of a farmer's plough that is used to turn the earth over before planting seeds. (Show an image of the famous statue depicting this activity at the UN building in New York.) Read aloud Isaiah 2:3–4.

It's a powerful idea, and some peace campaigners still use it today. Weapons cost a great deal of money to design and make, and Britain still makes a lot of money selling weapons around the world. Wouldn't it be better to spend all that time and effort on something that sustains life instead of taking it away? Imagine what it would be like if we could take weapons of war and turn them into something beautiful or useful! Then show images of the *Throne of Weapons* or *Tree of Life* artworks produced with guns salvaged from the Mozambique civil war, from http://learn.christianaid.org.uk/TeachersResources/secondary/weapons_english.aspx.

Ask your pupils to create a new artwork entitled *Turning Swords into Ploughshares*, using images of swords, rifles, tanks or warplanes. Online clip-art collections provide useful cartoon-style imagery. The artwork could be a 2D or 3D collage or an ICT project. Could these images now be used to create a design for a flower, a pram, a bicycle or some other peaceful thing? What is the key message about weapons that your pupils would want the artwork to convey? Could you say this without words? Ensure that your pupils spend time visualising and drafting the end result before starting their image search.

Literacy: Writing about peace and war

Age 5–7: Writing about a peaceful world

With your class, discuss and list the things that happen in the world that make them feel sad. Explain that 'peace' can mean all sorts of things. It's not simply 'nothing happening'. It could mean that everything is good and people are being treated fairly. What sorts of things would we want to see happening? How would people have to be different? What would it be like to live in a world like that? Set your class the task of writing about 'One day in a peaceful world'. What would they see and hear happening on the way to school?

Age 8–11: Writing about the hymn 'I vow to thee, my country'

Song lyrics can reveal a great deal about beliefs and values. Play a recording of Gustav Holst's 'Jupiter' from *The Planets*. Explain that after the First World War, the slow movement of this piece was used as the tune for a popular new hymn. You can find the lyrics and the story behind them here: http://en.wikipedia.org/wiki/I_Vow_to_Thee,_My_Country.

Point out that the second verse isn't used nowadays. Can your pupils see any references in it to the First World War? Show an image of 'Britannia', sourced from Google Images, to illustrate 'my country'. Now look at the first verse of the hymn. What do we think about someone promising to love their own country like that? (It's called 'patriotism'.) A sacrifice is about giving up something really important—maybe their own life. Do they think it is right to offer to die for their country? What questions would they have for a person who loved their country in this way?

Then consider the third verse. This refers to the Christian idea of the kingdom of God, as described by Jesus. Read it through. Why do they think the author has spent verse 1 talking about loving his country, verse 2 about dying for it, and verse 3 talking about God's invisible kingdom of peace?

Discuss pupils' responses to the song and their questions about what it is saying, and then whether they like it or not. (Some people now wish the song had never been written: they just want to enjoy the tune without thinking of the words. What do you think about that?) Now, imagine that your school has been asked to put together a choir to perform the song as part of a special concert remembering the First World War. Would you be happy to sing all these words or not? Write a letter to the concert organiser, explaining your reactions to the song's ideas and messages, and give your reasons why you do or don't wish to sing the words.

Numeracy: Counting the human cost

Age 7–11: Looking at casualty numbers

It can be jaw-dropping to consider the human cost of large-scale conflicts. The casualty statistics from the First World War lend themselves to thoughtful tasks with data handling, presentation techniques using graphs and tables, and work on percentages. Depending on a class's general grasp of place value, a teacher may need to do some rounding of figures first to make the task easier. The raw data can be found on websites such as http://en.wikipedia. org/wiki/World_War_I_casualties.

First, spend some time looking at the figures. Check the column headings. Note how some figures may be suspiciously rounded already, because nobody was able (or bothering) to keep a close tally. Note also the contrasts between the number of military deaths, the number of military wounded and the number of civilian deaths in different countries (for example, France and Britain). Enquiries such as the following may spark some revealing answers:

• Which countries of the British Empire had the greatest casualties among their armed forces?

- Which of Britain's allies suffered the greatest casualties?
- Compare these numbers with the figures for the 'Central Powers', including the German Empire.
- Which countries lost the greatest numbers of civilians?
- Which countries lost the greatest percentage of their overall population?
- What other questions do the numbers suggest for you?

Consider the numbers of people wounded in a country. How would it affect the country afterwards, if many of its young men had been injured in war? If you were the leader of that country, what challenges might be facing you? What decisions might you have to make?

Citizenship: Remembering the sacrifice of others

Age 5–11: Studying local heroes

Most localities in the British Isles will feature at least one war memorial. Many are placed in the grounds or buildings of local parish churches; others can be found in town centres, near crossroads, at central railway stations and many other places. Find out where they are, using the website www.ukniwm.org.uk, then consider planning a study trip for your class to see a memorial, sketch it and find out the names of those people whose lives are commemorated there. What images and symbols are used in the memorial? What materials are used? When was it created? What accompanying words are used to explain the significance of the place? Are there any words or phrases taken from the Bible or some other text? What do you notice about the names and ranks of the people listed? Have any of their stories been researched by local historians? (Your local library may know.)

An extremely useful resource on this theme is the *English Parish Church through the Centuries* DVD-ROM, which provides a wealth of information about English parish churches and their history. The accompanying primary schools' pack is available as a free download, with fully illustrated lesson plans, worksheets and assemblies. This is a real asset to anyone planning a school trip to a local parish church. Go to www.christianityandculture.org.uk/education/primary-schools-pack.

Age 9–11: Finding out about prisoners of conscience

Amnesty International campaigns on behalf of prisoners of conscience today. Their website contains useful lesson plans about human rights for upper primary school children: visit the teachers' pages at www.amnesty.org.uk.

Personal and Social Education/Circle Time: Peacemakers

Age 5–11: Resolving conflict

Ask your pupils: 'When did you last get really cross with another child in school? What happened? How did it feel? How was it sorted out?' Explain that people can get angry about all sorts of things. Sometimes it is one person having a go at someone else, and sometimes it can be two people who just don't get on. Then it blows up and things are said that shouldn't be said, and things are done that shouldn't be done, and everything goes sour. What happens then? What's the best way to sort out these arguments? (Discuss in pairs, then feed back.)

It can be helpful to have someone else (a mediator) to listen to both sides and make them listen to each other, to see if the problem can be sorted out instead of getting worse. Mediators can sort out a lot of situations. (Of course, if you're being bullied, you should tell a responsible adult; you can't 'sort things out' if somebody enjoys being horrible to you.)

Role-play a situation of conflict. Get into threes and decide who will be characters A, B and C. (Ask one group of three to stand up, to make the different roles clear.) Explain that A is cross because B won't let them join in a game, so B is keeping A from playing with their friends. B is the one organising the game and is fed up with the way A tries to keep taking it over, changing the rules and messing things up. A and B have started saying horrible things to each other, and are both angry. C is the mediator. C's job is to hear what A and B are saying, make them listen to each other, and try to find a way through that satisfies both of them. Sit in triplets facing each other. Spend a few moments imagining yourselves into the roles, and then start talking.

Afterwards, ask for feedback on what happened. Ask pupils who they were playing and how it felt. Were there any successful attempts by mediators to sort it all out? Discuss them. Point out that this is called peacemaking, and learning to do it well is very important.

THOUGHT FOR THE DAY

Jesus said: 'Blessed are the peacemakers, for they will be called children of God.'
MATTHEW 5:9 (NIV)

Prayer

Father God, thank you for everyone who works hard to sort out our problems. Help me to learn to be a peacemaker too. Amen

Assemblies

— ASSEMBLY 1 —

How the 'Great War' started

This assembly attempts to explain how the First World War began, using the imagery of a playground fight. It will require the services of a range of willing and confident pupils who can be relied on to act responsibly and improvise safely. (Alternatively, the whole thing could be a pre-rehearsed production.) The story is necessarily simplified and you may wish to change parts of it to suit your own political perspective, but do try to maintain a balance. The aim is to show how getting into a fight can have unintended consequences, a lesson that is true as much for adults as it is for children.

Preparation

You will need 22 hats marked with the names of the various countries involved. The simplest method is to make a set of hatbands from strips of card to fit a variety of different-sized heads (experiment beforehand on some willing children), with an extra strip to go over the top of the head. On the front of each hatband, staple the name of a country, written large. You'll need the following: Britain and Ireland (one hat), Germany, Austria-Hungary, France, Belgium (for a small child), Serbia, Turkey, Russia, Italy, Japan, Australia, India, New Zealand, Canada, South Africa, Bulgaria, USA, Austria, Hungary, Czechoslovakia, Poland, Republic of Ireland.

If you can, sit your audience 'in the round' so that you can place your countries in geographical locations, with Austria-Hungary in the middle. When the countries 'fight', they should not move around but instead shadow-box, not touching each other. Have a 'silence' signal established at the beginning so that everyone can quieten down to hear you say what happens next.

Introduction

A hundred years ago, the most powerful nations in the world fell out with each other and went to war. At the time, it seemed so terrible and awful that they called it the 'Great War', the 'war to end all wars'. Sadly, it wasn't, because there have been many wars since then, but this one was the first that seemed to drag in just about every country around the world, and it changed everything. It broke up some old countries and created new ones. It brought many terrible new weapons into use and millions of people died, both on the battlefield and away from it. Every family in this country was affected by it in some way, and life was never the same again.

Looking deeper

How did it start? Perhaps the best way we can explain it is by doing some acting. We need some children who are happy to come and do a bit of acting in front of everyone else. *(Place Austria-Hungary, Germany, Serbia, Russia, France, Belgium and Britain-and-Ireland in roughly geographical locations in the performance area, with Austria-Hungary in the 'middle' and others placed accordingly nearby. The other players need to be sitting towards both sides, ready to be brought in later.)* Once upon a time, a hundred years ago, there were some really powerful nations.

Britain and Ireland said, 'I'm the greatest!'

Then France, then Russia, then Austria-Hungary, then Turkey, all said 'No, I'm the greatest!' one after another.

But then there was Germany, a new country, who said, 'I need to be the greatest, too!'

So they all argued with each other about who was the greatest. *(All argue, pointing to each other.)*

After a time, they started to gang up on each other.

France said, 'Who's going to be in my gang?' Russia said, 'Me!' and stood by France. Great Britain said, 'Me… sort of…' and also stood by France.

Austria-Hungary said, 'Who's going to be in my gang?' Germany and Turkey said, 'Me!' and stood together. They called themselves 'the Central Powers'.

Then a cross little nation called Serbia (*bring on a new child with hat*), which was part of Austria-Hungary, said, 'I don't want to be part of this gang! I want to be in my own gang!'

Austria-Hungary (*looking rather menacing*) said, 'Keep quiet, you little shrimp, or else!'

But then Russia said, 'Oi! Leave him alone! He's my mate! Pick on somebody your own size!'

Austria-Hungary said, 'Mind your own business, Russia!'

Russia said, 'Don't make me angry! I'll be terrible if I get angry!'

Germany said, 'Oi, Russia! Leave Austria-Hungary alone! He's my mate!'

France said to Germany, 'Oi! You leave Russia alone! He's my mate!'

Turkey said, 'What's going on?'

Britain and Ireland said, 'What's Germany up to? I don't trust him one bit.'

Germany said, 'And you can mind your own business too!'

France said to Britain and Ireland, 'They're ganging up on me!'

Britain and Ireland said to France, 'Calm down, nothing's going to happen. We're friends, aren't we?'

Then Serbia gave Austria-Hungary a punch on the nose, and Austria-Hungary said, 'Right! That does it!' and started fighting him.

Russia said, 'Right! That does it!' and started fighting Austria-Hungary.

Germany said, 'Now what? I've got Russia and France ganging up on me! I'd better knock out France quickly!' and started fighting France. But standing in the way was a little country called Belgium (*bring on a new child with hat*), who said, 'Heeeeeelp!'

Britain and Ireland said, 'I'll rescue you, Belgium!' and joined in the fight as well.

Then some other countries joined in. (*Introduce new hats to children, who stay around the edge of the circle.*) Bulgaria, India, South Africa, Canada, New Zealand, Australia, Italy, Japan and the USA all started picking sides and fighting too.

Russia went a bit crazy, turning around in circles. 'What's going on? I can't handle all this! I'm having a revolution!' and stopped fighting.

(*Everybody sits down quietly.*) The fight went on for a very long time. Everyone was getting badly hurt. Finally they stopped, exhausted, and all the other countries (the Allies) pointed at the 'Central Powers' of Germany, Austria-Hungary and Turkey and Bulgaria to say, 'It's all your fault!' Naturally they replied, 'Oh no, it isn't!' (Loud choruses of 'Oh, yes, it is!' 'Oh no, it isn't!' 'Well, you started it!' 'No, we didn't! You did!' 'No, you did!' 'You did!' and so on.)

The Allies had won, so they decided to punish the countries they'd beaten.

Germany (*stand up*) was told to pay for everybody's hospital expenses. 'Pay up!' they all said. Turkey and Bulgaria had to pay up too. (*Loud cries from the Central Powers of 'It's not fair! I'll get you for this!'*)

Austria-Hungary was told it couldn't be a country any more and was broken up into lots of little countries (*bring on new children with hats, such as Czechoslovakia, Austria, Poland and Hungary, saying, 'Help! I'm falling apart! It's not fair!'*)

But after the fight, the Allies had their problems too. Most of Ireland (*bring on a new child with hat*) said it didn't want to be British any more. (*'Fight your own battles in future!'*)

India, South Africa, Canada, New Zealand and Australia all said, 'I hope that was worth it. Er... it was worth it, wasn't it?' Some of them weren't too sure. It had been a very nasty fight. The USA said, 'I don't trust any of you at all!' and went home for his tea.

By the end, all the countries were cross and unhappy and bruised and fed up. Nothing had really been sorted out, and they just knew there'd be another fight before long. There was: we call it the Second World War. That was even worse.

Now, we've told this story as if it was the story of some children getting into a horrible fight. What do you think started it? What were the biggest mistakes? Was there one country to blame, or more than one? (*Encourage a short time of pupil discussion, then feed back a few answers.*)

Two thousand years ago, one of Jesus' friends wrote this:

Where do you think all these appalling wars and quarrels come from? Do you think they just happen? Think again. They come about because you want your own way, and fight for it deep inside yourselves. You lust for what you don't have and are willing to kill to get it. You want what isn't yours and will risk violence to get your hands on it. You wouldn't think of just asking God for it, would you? And why not? Because you know you'd be asking for what you have no right to. You're spoiled children, each wanting your own way. (James 4:1–3, THE MESSAGE)

When you look at the mess of the First World War, these words sound true. The fight led to millions of families being hurt all around the world, because so many people were killed or injured.

People can get into fights for all sorts of reasons but it usually comes down to someone being selfish or greedy—and someone always ends up getting hurt. So next time you feel you want something really badly and you think that nothing's going to stand in your way, think again. Think things through. All these countries didn't start out wanting to go to war, but that's what happened in the end. Next time you get cross about something, stop. Take a deep breath. Count to ten. Talk about it. Try to sort things out. Try to get on with everyone, even the ones you don't like, because once people start fighting, you never know how it's going to end.

THOUGHT FOR THE DAY

Think of something you get angry about. Imagine holding it in your fist, as tight as you can. Then... relax your hand. Let the thing go. Imagine it drifting away, up into the air. It's OK to be angry, but it's not OK to let your anger control you, so if you're angry about something, talk about it to someone who can help.

'Sin is when you treat people as things. Including yourself. That's what sin is.'
TERRY PRATCHETT, *CARPE JUGULUM*

Prayer

Father God, help me to learn from the mistakes of others, so that I don't have to make their mistakes all over again. Amen

— ASSEMBLY 2 —

The creation of the Unknown Soldier

The religious concept of sacrifice is unfamiliar to many pupils but it is a key element in understanding how people of the time thought about those who died in the First World War. The 'IHS' seen on many crosses (a short form of the name 'Jesus' in Greek) stood in the minds of many for a different message: 'I have suffered'. What might that sacrifice mean for us now?

Preparation

You will need to display an image of the Unknown Soldier's tomb in Westminster Abbey.

Introduction

How good are you at remembering things? Can you remember what you had for lunch yesterday, or last Saturday? Can you remember what the weather was like last Tuesday? Can you remember what you were doing in Literacy last week on Monday? When we remember things, we're pulling together our memories of what happened, but there's more to memory than just keeping a record of what we've done. Computers need memory to work things out and handle new software, and, if they don't have enough memory, that means they lack the processing power to carry out jobs. Of course, you can buy extra memory for computers and other devices. Could you buy extra memory for people?

In a way, you can. Our brains are designed to handle all sorts of tasks and we can add to our processing power in here *(tap head)* by asking questions and finding out new things. The more we make interesting connections between different bits of knowledge—in history, literacy, RE and all the other things we learn in school—the more we understand and the more our minds can do.

So what's Remembrance Sunday all about? It's about pulling memories together—memories of other people—finding out their stories and piecing it all together in our heads. Remembrance Sunday is the day when we remember all those who died in wars around the world. That's a big thing to think about—maybe too big—but it helps if we focus on a few stories that can stand for all the others. Here's a very important story that has helped a lot of people to understand what happened in the First World War 100 years ago. It's about keeping a memory alive in a very special way.

Looking deeper

David Railton was a chaplain in the British Army, a priest who travelled and lived with the soldiers as they went into battle, helping to keep up spirits and care for the wounded. Soldiers need someone like that to be there for them when things get tough. David was that kind of chaplain and later he received a medal, the Military Cross, for his bravery. This story, though, is about something else he did.

One evening, he had just finished burying another soldier, saying some last words as the man's friends stood around the grave. David had been doing a lot of that lately. His regiment had just taken over an old French farmhouse for their officers to sleep in, so, when he got back, everything seemed quiet—but then, round the back of the farmhouse, in the garden, he saw another grave. Afterwards, he wrote:

At the head of the grave there stood a rough cross of white wood. On the cross was written in deep, black-pencilled letters, 'An Unknown British soldier… of the Black Watch' (a Scottish regiment). It was dusk, and no one was near… I remember how still it was. Even the guns seemed to be resting. How that grave gave me to think! How I wondered! How I longed to see his folk! But who was he, and who were they? … Quietly and gradually there came out of the mist of thought this answer, clear and strong. 'Let this body—this symbol of him—be carried reverently over the sea to his native land.'

Slowly, a big idea started to grow in David's head. After the war, he shared the idea: could we bury an unknown soldier in Westminster Abbey in the heart of London, alongside all the famous soldiers? That way, anybody who had lost a husband, a father or a son in the war and didn't know what had happened could come to the Abbey and think that maybe the lost one was there, gone but not forgotten. The idea spread. Letters were written, committees met, and the answer was 'Yes'. They would do it in time for Armistice Day, 11 November 1920.

Here's where the story gets a bit strange. They had to find an unknown soldier to bury. Across the battlefields of France and Belgium, there were lots of buried soldiers with no names. Which one would they choose? Four bodies were dug up and placed in fresh coffins, and one was selected. No one knew his name. He could have been English, Irish, Scots, Indian, Australian, Canadian or South African—anyone who fought in British uniform. The body was brought back to Britain with special parades and ceremonies, then finally lowered into the specially made tomb in the Abbey. On top of the coffin, the King scattered soil from the battlefield. David's big idea of the Unknown Soldier had finally come home, a symbol and reminder of all those who had died.

So what? Does it matter now? It depends. You might have a family connection—a great-great-grandparent who was caught up in the fighting. The First World War shaped a lot of our modern world, and that's worth trying to understand. We still have armed forces serving in dangerous places, and every so often they get badly injured or killed. They and their families still need to be cared for or remembered. That matters.

Jesus said, 'Greater love has no one than this: to lay down one's life for one's friends' (John 15:13, TNIV). That's a big idea. Why would anyone put their life on the line for someone else, making a sacrifice, paying the price? Would you do it? I don't know if I could, but many people have done it in real life—and that is still amazing, whether it happened yesterday or 100 years ago or even 2,000 years ago. Christians believe that Jesus did it, dying on the cross.

Of course, making a sacrifice isn't just about life or death. People are always giving things up for the sake of others. They might give up their time or their comfort so that someone else can have a better life. Sacrifices can come in all shapes and sizes. Has somebody ever sacrificed something for you? Are you thankful for it? Could you be thankful if somebody you didn't know sacrificed something for you? That's an even bigger question!

THOUGHT FOR THE DAY

Everything we're going to be given today will happen because someone else takes the trouble to give it. The things we get to do in school, the food we eat at lunch time, the homes we go back to at the end of the day, are all there because someone else took the trouble to make them happen. Try to say, 'Thank you' for them today.

Prayer

Lord Jesus, thank you for everyone who's ever given something up so that I can live my life well. I might know their names, or not, but thank you anyway. Amen

*

The Christmas truce

The tale of the unofficial 'peace' in December 1914 has been retold many times, but why does the 'Christmas truce' resonate so deeply with audiences today? This assembly tries to explore that deeper meaning.

Preparation

Using Google Images, you may want to show some pictures connected with the events and, if you can find one, an old-fashioned brown leather football.

Introduction

There's a very famous story from the First World War about what happened during the Christmas of 1914 as British, French and German soldiers faced each other from their trenches across No Man's Land. It was winter, the first winter of the war, and it was very cold and wet, with a lot of ice and snow. The soldiers on both sides hadn't expected to be spending Christmas standing in a hole in the middle of a muddy field. They'd all thought the war would be over by then, but it was harder and nastier than anyone had expected. The soldiers had thought they would be charging around on horses and fighting the enemy in fast, furious battles. Instead, everything had slowed down. You can't charge around on horses when there are machine guns and barbed wire against you. Instead, you dig your hole in the ground and try not to get shot too quickly.

So there they all were, on Christmas Eve.

Somewhere along the line, some German soldiers started singing Christmas carols in their trenches. Every German unit had been given traditional Christmas trees to decorate. Perhaps it reminded them of home. When they heard the singing, some British soldiers in their trenches cheered and sang a few songs back. Then something crazy happened.

Looking deeper

Let's imagine one of those soldiers could tell us about it. What might they say?

* * *

I just don't believe it! Yesterday we were shooting at each other. Last night we started singing Christmas carols at each other, and today we've been playing football. It all started this morning when one of the officers from the other side came over waving a white flag and said, 'Shall we have a truce, just for today? Shall we celebrate Christmas by not fighting?' And our officers said, 'Well… all right.'

So we sent out stretcher parties to pick up the dead, because that's important, and so did the Germans. There we are in the cold, looking for bodies in uniform—our khaki and their field-grey. Sometimes we'd point them out to the others, to be helpful: 'There's one of yours over here.' Gently, we'd collect our friends, dig graves and bury them, and the funny thing is, when it came to having a funeral service for our dead friends, we sort of joined up with the Germans. We all took off our hats and a chaplain said prayers for the dead. I think we were praying for the dead of both sides, which is strange because we'd just been shooting them. And now we were all together, trying to clear up the mess. After that, someone got out a bottle to share. We started swapping badges.

Then things went a bit crazy. Someone just had to bring out… a football. A football! England versus Germany! What could go wrong? You should have seen us—20-a-side, 40-a-side, it didn't matter. What a match! Amazing tackles. Fantastic saves. Unbelievable goals. There were 30, 40, 50, 60 of us all slipping and sliding in the mud, and it was fun. (They still beat us on penalties, though.)

Afterwards, one of the Germans came up to me and said in English, 'All right, mate?' He sounded like a Londoner. He got out some photos. 'What are you doing fighting for them?' I asked. 'My mum married a German and we lived in London till I was 15. Then we moved to Germany, and, when the war started, I signed up to fight for my new country. So here I am.' He showed me photos of his family and I showed him photos of mine back home.

As it got dark, we lit a fire and sang some songs together in English and German, promised not to do any shooting on Boxing Day, and went back to our own trenches. A few days later, we were fighting again.'

* * *

It's a strange story. In the middle of a war, peace broke out. It wasn't true all along the line. Some soldiers carried on fighting during Christmas 1914, and others had their truce over New Year. When the generals in charge on both sides heard about it, they were really angry and put a stop to it. All the soldiers who'd stopped fighting were quickly moved to other places along the line in case they got too friendly with the enemy again.

So why is it still remembered? Why do you think people still tell this story? What does it do for us? (*Ask pupils to discuss it with a partner, then feed back a few responses.*)

It's good to know that people can choose to stop fighting. It's good to know that when people fall out with each other, it doesn't have to carry on for ever: we can still come together and remember the good things we do share. I wonder, could it happen now, in this school? In our playground? In our homes? What would it take to make it happen? Has it got to be someone else who makes the first move? Think of that first soldier who decided to try to cross No Man's Land. It must have been pretty scary. It must have taken a lot of courage to make the first move. Where's your No Man's Land, the place you don't want to go? Where's that place where you've been at war with someone?

Here's a weird thought. Christians believe that on the very first Christmas, God stepped into No Man's Land by coming as Jesus into a dangerous place, our world, to say to the whole human race, 'Let's be friends.' Jesus coming out to greet people in No Man's Land—what do you think about *that*?

THOUGHT FOR THE DAY

Let there be peace on earth—and let it begin with me.

Prayer

Father God, show me the places where I could make peace with people. Show me how to make peace with them in a way that's fair to everybody, including me. But above everything, show me how to care for people as people you have made, every one of them infinitely precious. Amen

Extension ideas

- One man has had the crazy idea to hold a World Peace Day, when wars could stop for just one day, every 21 September. He's had some interesting successes: see http://peaceoneday. org/welcome
- For an original newspaper report of the Christmas truce, see www.theguardian.com/theguardian/from-the-archive-blog/2011/dec/23/from-the-archive-blog-christmas-truce-1914

*

Acknowledgements and sources

Tommy's Ark by Richard van Emden (Bloomsbury, 2010).

Alarms and Excursions: Reminiscences of a soldier by Lieutenant-General Sir Tom Bridges (Longmans, Green and Co., 1938).

To End All Wars by Adam Hochschild (Macmillan, 2011).

Keir Hardie by Emrys Hughes (Allen and Unwin, 1956).

Indian Voices of the Great War: Soldiers' letters, 1914–18, selected and introduced by David Omissi (Macmillan Press, 1999).

Woodbine Willie: An Anglican Incident by William Purcell (Hodder and Stoughton, 1962).

The Naturalist and the Christ by Tim Heaton (Circle Books, 2011).

Virtual History: Alternatives and counterfactuals by Niall Ferguson (ed.) (Papermac, 1998).

Forgotten Voices of the Great War by Max Arthur (Ebury Press, 2002).

William Coltman: The story of two crosses by Anthony G. Tideswell (Sovereign Bookcare, 2008).

'The Attack' by Richard H. Tawney, published in the *Westminster Gazette*, August 1916, republished in *The Attack and Other Papers* (Allen and Unwin, 1953).

The Roses of No Man's Land by Lyn MacDonald (Penguin, 1980).

The Unknown Soldier by Neil Hanson (Doubleday, 2005).

God On Our Side: The British padre in World War I by Michael Moynihan (Leo Cooper, 1983).

Barnabas RE Days

Exploring Christianity creatively

A Barnabas RE Day is a full day's visit to your school to bring the Bible to life for primary-aged children through a range of the creative arts. The Barnabas Children's Ministry team explores themes which address many PSHE/Citizenship objectives. The sessions use different creative arts according to the particular skills of the team member undertaking your booking, such as storytelling, music, dance, mime, drama, creative writing or drawing. The material is based on biblical and historical accounts, personal story and shared experience. The timetable, class groupings and themes are completely flexible and will be organised between you and the Barnabas ministry team to suit your school's needs.

For more information, contact the Barnabas Team Administrator on 01865 319704 or email barnabas@brf.org.uk. You can also visit the website: www.barnabasinschools.org.uk.

What Price Peace? Barnabas RE Days

From a very early age, children are impacted by media images of war and violent conflict. BRF's Barnabas RE Day for Foundation Stage, Key Stage 1 and Key Stage 2 uses the 100th anniversary of the First World War to explore issues surrounding war, peace and reconciliation in a creative and thought-provoking way. Is it a case of 'My country, right or wrong', or are there bigger questions to face? Through a combination of real-life accounts from the First World War and older insights into conflict and peacemaking from the Christian Bible, this workshop uses the experiences and insights of the past to illuminate similar issues in our modern world.

About the author

Chris Hudson is part of BRF's Barnabas Children's Ministry team. An experienced teacher, author and trainer, dedicated to promoting high quality teaching and learning in primary schools, he provides regular INSET for schools on a variety of themes related to the Bible and Christianity, together with Barnabas RE Day storytelling, drama and music workshops for schoolchildren.

Christianity: Key Beliefs and Traditions

An RE resource for teaching Christianity at Key Stage 2

Cavan Wood

Christianity: Key Beliefs and Traditions is an essential resource for teaching Christianity at Key Stage 2. It seeks to inform and equip RE teachers by looking at key theological ideas such as creation and salvation as well as at the life of Jesus and the growth of the church. Over 30 topics are covered, each including background information, classroom activities and learning objectives. The emphasis is not just on the history of Christianity but on the Christian faith as it is lived now and on evaluating its key ideas, linking themes to pupils' experience and understanding.

Free template downloads are also available to accompany the book.

ISBN 978 0 85746 251 0   £7.99
Available from your local Christian bookshop or direct from BRF: please visit www.barnabasinschools.org.uk.

Enjoyed

this book?

Write a review—we'd love to hear what you think.
Email: reviews@brf.org.uk

Keep up to date—receive details of our new books as they happen.
Sign up for email news and select your interest groups at:
www.brfonline.org.uk/findoutmore/

Follow us on Twitter @brfonline

By post—to receive new title information by post (UK only), complete the form below and post to: BRF Mailing Lists, 15 The Chambers, Vineyard, Abingdon, Oxfordshire, OX14 3FE

Your Details
Name _____
Address_____
_____
Town/City _____ Post Code _____
Email _____

Your Interest Groups (*Please tick as appropriate)	
☐ Advent/Lent	☐ Messy Church
☐ Bible Reading & Study	☐ Pastoral
☐ Children's Books	☐ Prayer & Spirituality
☐ Discipleship	☐ Resources for Children's Church
☐ Leadership	☐ Resources for Schools

Support your local bookshop
Ask about their new title information schemes.